W9-CFA-536

LANTERN PRESS BOOKS

are complete and unabridged reprints of titles in the several series of thematic short-story anthologies published originally by Lantern Press, Inc. Over two million copies have been sold in their higher-priced, cloth-bound editions.

Teachers, librarians, and reviewers have often recommended these carefully edited anthologies. For instance, *Scholastic Teacher* said: "All are suitable as supplementary readers for junior high school students. Each title appears on most school and library approved reading lists and is recommended by *The Library Journal*. Though mainly for junior high school readers, they can be read with pleasure by older students and they are endorsed by Spache in GOOD READING FOR POOR READERS."

A complete list of the titles now available will be found on the reverse side of this page. If your bookseller doesn't have a title you want, you can get it by sending retail price, local sales tax if any, plus 25¢ (50¢ if you order two or more books) for postage and handling to Mail Service Department, POCKET BOOKS, a Division of Simon & Schuster, Inc., 1 West 39th Street, New York, N.Y. 10018. If you are ordering for delivery in Canada, send retail price plus 25¢ (50¢ if you order two or more books) for postage and handling to Simon & Schuster of Canada, Ltd., 330 Steelcase Road, Markham, Ontario. In either case, please send check or money order. We cannot be responsible for cash.

Now Available:

BASEBALL STORIES 68017/95¢
DOG STORIES 68012/95¢
FOOTBALL STORIES 80677/$1.25
GHOST STORIES 68024/95¢
GRIDIRON STORIES 55166/60¢
HAUNTED STORIES 75841/75¢
HORSE STORIES 80632/$1.25
MORE DOG STORIES 68014/95¢
MORE GHOST STORIES 75845/75¢
MORE HAUNTED STORIES 77712/95¢
MORE HORSE STORIES 80378/$1.25
MYSTERY STORIES 80410/$1.25
OUTER SPACE STORIES 80620/$1.25
RESCUE STORIES 75775/75¢
SCIENCE FICTION STORIES 75750/75¢
SPACE ADVENTURES 75843/75¢
SUSPENSE STORIES 75747/75¢
UNDERWATER ADVENTURE STORIES 75730/75¢

FOOTBALL STORIES

(Original title: *More Teen-Age Football Stories*)

Edited by
JOSH FURMAN

A LANTERN
PRESS BOOK

PUBLISHED BY POCKET BOOKS NEW YORK

FOOTBALL STORIES

Lantern Press edition published September, 1976

This POCKET BOOK edition is printed from brand-new plates
made from completely reset, clear, easy to-read type.
POCKET BOOK editions are published by POCKET BOOKS,
a division of Simon & Schuster, Inc.,
A GULF+WESTERN COMPANY
630 Fifth Avenue,
New York, N.Y. 10020.
Trademarks registered in the United States
and other countries.

ISBN: 0-671-80677-7.
Library of Congress Catalog Card Number: 74-21888.
This Lantern Press edition is published by arrangement with
Lantern Press, Inc. Copyright, ©, 1975, by Lantern Press, Inc.
"Dark, Dank and Dismal," by Wade H. Mosby, copyright,
©, 1961, by the Boy Scouts of America, reprinted by permis-
sion of Larry Sternig Literary Agency; "The Fullback from
Liechtenstein," by Jack Ritchie, copyright, ©, 1963, by the
Boy Scouts of America, reprinted by permission of Larry
Sternig Literary Agency; "The Almost Magic Toe," by Jack
Ritchie, copyright, ©, 1966, by George A. Pflaum Publisher,
Inc., reprinted by permission of Larry Sternig Literary
Agency. All rights reserved. *Football Stories* was originally
published under the title *More Teen-Age Football Stories.*
This book, or portions thereof, may not be reproduced by
any means without permission of the original publisher:
Lantern Press, Inc., 354 Hussey Road, Mount Vernon,
New York 10522.

Printed in the U.S.A.

Contents

Football Stories

Roar with Roark

❖━━❖━━❖━━❖

ARTHUR TOFTE

AS any high school grandstand quarterback can tell you, it takes incentive to win football games. But what kind of incentive does it take to lose?

Don't ask me. I'm the kind that likes to win, not lose.

That's why I groaned to myself as I sat in the top row in the Stadium watching the game with Dunlap. Roark—that's my school—was losing again.

Not only that—both the team and the student body seemed to *want* to lose!

For over seven long, weary years Roark had been losing. The national record for consecutive losses by a high school team had long since been broken. Now every defeat added to that dismal record. In fact, Roark hadn't scored a point in almost three years.

1

You guessed it!

What it did was put our little old Roark high school on the sports map—in a reverse sort of way of course. I suppose there are twisted minds that think if you can't be the best, be the worst.

Well, Roark was the worst. Sports writers from coast to coast delighted in writing up our games. Always comically. Big joke. It gave them a chance to show how clever they could be.

And wherever football fans gathered, all anyone had to do was say the magic word "Roark" and everybody present would burst out into laughter.

Not so surprising, every game was a sellout. People—I won't call them fans—came from the whole southern half of the state to pull for another Roark defeat, for bigger and funnier misplays.

You'd think that pride in one's school had gone out of fashion.

But not with me.

I'm Vic Talbot. Just "Vic" Talbot. All my life, all sixteen years of it, I have dreamed of being called "Young Iron Vic."

There's an "Iron Vic" tradition at Roark High. Back in 1919, the first year of the Lake Conference, Roark won the championship behind the running of "Iron Vic" Talbot, my grandfather. He played every minute of every game, scored all the team's points, and was acclaimed

2

the state's top high school fullback his last two years.

That was the start of the "Iron Vic" tradition.

My father continued the custom right after the Second World War. Not as big as my grandfather, he was Roark's most famous end. He broke all records for catching touchdown passes and still holds Roark's record for total points scored in a season. He too played every minute of every game. There was never any doubt about his right to bear the title of "Iron Vic the Second."

But I'm not the "Iron Vic" of my generation. You see, when I was twelve, I was in a car accident. My father lost his life. I lost my left arm, and with it my chance to be another "Iron Vic." One-armed football players are about as rare as one-armed pole vaulters.

Anyway, here I was watching the hapless Roark team stumbling through missed tackles, fumbles, interceptions, offside fouls, errors upon errors in its game with Dunlap, one of the weakest schools in the Conference.

At the moment, Roark was with its back to the wall on its own five yard line. The quarterback tossed the ball toward a flanker. The back turned the wrong way. The ball went floating past him into the end zone. A Dunlap lineman was diving for it. I couldn't look any more.

Instead of looking—and hereby hangs the tale—I turned my head away.

I could tell by the roar of the crowd that Dun-

3

lap had scored another touchdown on the fumble. I just didn't want to watch it.

I looked off over the tree-covered park behind the Stadium. It was part of what made the town of Roark so picturesque and lovely. The foliage was just beginning to turn into its gaudy autumnal colors. The grass had still its summer green.

But something else out there caught my eye.

Off in the far part of the park where we held our track meets, a tall, gangling youth was throwing a football all by himself. I turned all the way around and continued to watch.

He would grip the ball in one huge hand, rear back and let fly. Straight as a baseball it would speed toward a small stake he had driven into the ground seventy or eighty yards away. Then he would retrieve the ball and do it all over again.

There was something almost like poetry in the way he was throwing that football—the sureness of it, the deadly aim, the tremendous distance.

I knew instantly who it was. Everybody at Roark knew him. It was Rod Duncan, our star basketball center. He was six feet ten and still growing. Roark might be a joke in football. But not in basketball. Not as long as Rod was on our team.

If only Rod could play football—with that forward passing ability!

Then I had this crazy idea.

We're a small school and a lot of our boys play both football and basketball. Even track, too. But

4

even though Coach Pennscott handled all three sports, he would never have permitted Rod to play football. Rod was a beanpole. One hard tackle would break him in half.

But then, as I said, I had this crazy, crazy idea.

Without taking another glance at the pathetic debacle down on the football field, I left the Stadium. I made my way across the park to where Rod was still practicing his throws.

"Hi, Rod," I said. "You toss that ball pretty well."

He grinned good-naturedly.

I'm nearly six feet tall, but I had to look up to him. I jerked my thumb in disgust at the sounds from the Stadium. "Even little Dunlap is rubbing it in," I said.

"Yeah, sickening isn't it?"

"Say," I said, "how would you like to help Roark beat Linden next Saturday?"

Linden was last year's Conference champion and had practically its whole team back. He smiled.

"What do you want me to do, put poison in their drinking water so they'll have to forfeit?"

"Yeah, something like that," I laughed. "Rod, sit down on this bench with me. I've got a real crazy idea."

Ten minutes later he nodded and said, "You were right, Vic. It's certainly a crazy idea. It's just crazy enough for me to agree to help."

Part of my plan, I must explain, was based on

5

the announcement made just before the game by Coach Pennscott that he was resigning unless Roark made some kind of effort to beat weak little Dunlap. Knowing the Coach, I had to count on it that that was exactly what he would do.

I went directly to my home. My grandfather, my mother and I live in a big old comfortable house only a block from school. Grandfather had made a lot of money when he was young. About ten years ago he had suffered a stroke and old "Iron Vic the First" was almost a total invalid. I loved my grandfather. I went right up to his room and told him about my crazy idea. At first he only glared at me with disbelief. Then the laugh lines around his eyes began to twitch. I knew he was ready to give me his backing.

That evening he called Mr. Spencer at his home. Mr. Spencer is our principal. Has been for a quarter century at least. Mr. Spencer agreed to see me.

I went straight over. He lived only about four blocks away. I guess I ran all the way.

After I told him my plan to help Roark beat Linden, he looked at me sternly. "Vic, I know you mean well. But your scheme is simply too crazy."

"That's just what my grandfather said—at first."

Mr. Spencer coughed in embarrassment. "You Talbots sure know how to apply pressure. Your grandfather gave me strict orders that I was to go along with your mad scheme. He even called

6

it that. But after he helped equip our science lab four years ago and gave us the swimming pool last year, I haven't the heart to refuse him—or you."

"You'll do it then?" I cried out eagerly.

He shrugged his shoulders. "I'm not even sure what you suggest is legal. We don't want to get kicked out of the Conference for violating rules."

"Grandfather says you have a whole week to work out the rules problems."

"All right, Vic. I'll try. What do you want me to do?"

I pondered for a moment. "Appoint my grandfather as Coach for the coming week. I'd like it in writing. Then, on Monday, I'll bring you a list of eleven boys in school. I would like you to do whatever the rules call for to make them eligible to play next Saturday. I'll make sure they are scholastically eligible. I'd like that list kept secret if you can manage it—at least until game time."

"That's all?" Mr. Spencer asked.

I nodded.

Immediately he sat down and wrote out a note saying that, with the resignation of Coach Pennscott, he was appointing Victor Talbot, Sr., as Coach *Pro Tem.*

I stuck the paper in my inner pocket and left.

Monday I searched out Bob Melton, Roark's fastest dash man. In last year's state high school track meet, he walked away with all the sprints. I mean, he ran away with them.

7

I told him my plan. Like all the rest, he was skeptical at first. Then he agreed. I told him what he had to do.

Tuesday I started around and talked to each boy that was on the list I had given Mr. Spencer. Each agreed to help.

After school on Tuesday, I went to the practice field where the team was listlessly going through scrimmage. Without a coach to tell them what to do, they seemed lost.

I walked out onto the field and picked up the football. The boys all stopped what they were doing and stared at me.

I pulled out the paper Mr. Spencer had written for me.

"I want you to know," I said, "that my grandfather, 'Iron Vic the First' is your new coach."

I went on, "And since he is even more unable to function than you seem to be, he has asked me to be his messenger today. He says to tell you there will be no need to practice this week."

Bull Stephens, the team's strongest running back, spoke up. "Come on, Vic. I know we've played lousy. But what chance do we have to get better if we don't practice?"

I looked at him. "We don't have much chance anyway, do we, Bull?"

I started to turn away. "Of course, if you want to go through some of the plays Coach Pennscott tried to teach you, I'm sure my grandfather

8

won't object. All he asks is that you get here at the Stadium Saturday in time to get suited up."

I could see that the boys were shocked. They knew that they had played poorly. But wasn't losing the name of the game at Roark? It had been a lark. They had been told they were making sports history.

I left them.

When Saturday noon came, I was as nervous as a cat with new kittens. The powerful, rawboned boys from Lindon had arrived and put in a limbering-up session on the playing field. The day was sunny and just cool enough.

I visited the Roark locker room. The boys had suited up. They looked at me questioningly.

Bull Stephens glanced around as though asking the others if he could speak for them.

"Without a coach, we feel kind of lost," he said.

"My grandfather is coach," I replied.

"But he isn't here."

"He'll be here. He'll be up there in the stands watching," I said flatly. With that I left them.

I walked over to the tool shed behind the Stadium. It was used by the groundskeeper. In it were my eleven very nervous boys, dressed in an assortment of old, discarded, very ill-fitting football uniforms.

"Look, fellows," I said, "you all know what you are to do. As soon as the coin tossing is over, I'll give you the signal to come out. I'm praying we win the toss."

"That may be the only thing we do win," one of the smallest of the boys piped up. "I'm praying we live through it."

If it hadn't been so tragic-serious, I would have laughed. This was surely the most pathetic, sickest football team ever to stumble over their own feet onto a football field. I winked bravely at Rod Duncan and Bill Melton and left.

Right on schedule the Linden team raced onto the field like a thundering herd. In contrast, the Roark team walked out slowly and sat down on the bench. They looked as though they wished they were anywhere but here.

I looked around at Mr. Spencer's roped-off reserved section on the fifty-yard line. I was relieved to see old "Iron Vic the First" there with a blanket around him.

The two captains went to the center of the field. The coin was tossed. I heaved a small sigh of relief when I saw that Roark had won the toss. We elected to receive.

I knew what a joke everybody expected out of the game. Appointing my invalid grandfather as coach was one thing. Then calling off the practice sessions only added to the ridiculousness of the situation.

The crowd was fully expecting to see a truly funny burlesque on the game of football that afternoon. I had heard that there were bets being made on just how many points Linden would score

10

on Roark in sixty minutes of play. All records were expected to be broken.

I looked for the head referee's signal that the teams should take the field.

Could my scheme work? Was it as crazy as everybody said? And yet I hardly dared think of the possibility of failure.

The Roark kick-off return team started to get up from the player's bench. I motioned them back.

Then I gave the signal to a boy I had stationed in the runway. He signaled to Rod Duncan who was standing in the doorway of the tool shed.

The noisy crowd suddenly hushed. Every head in the Stadium turned. Every pair of eyes stared with astonishment as my eleven misfits trotted out onto the field. How pathetically small they looked.

The school band which had been playing the school's victory song, *Roar with Roark,* stopped in the middle of a bar. The Linden players already on the field posed like statues in dumb amazement. Not a sound came from the stands. Our regular players sat on the bench as though stunned.

Then, like a dam breaking, the laughter burst forth in one great bellow. It shook the Stadium to its concrete foundation. People pounded each other on the back. Several of the Linden players sank to their knees in almost helpless hysterics.

11

Even the game officials made no attempt to retain their official dignity.

When some semblance of order had been restored, the Linden players lined up for the initial kick-off. The serious-faced, obviously scared Roark boys spread over their end of the field in haphazard fashion.

My instructions to them had been merely to ground the ball and not to try to run it back.

Apparently the Linden kicker was laughing too hard. His kick was not an especially good kick. The ball fell dead on the Roark nineteen yard line.

The crowd, sensing a highly dramatic bit of buffoonery, hushed its catcalls and whistles, and stood waiting for whatever madness was to occur.

The Roark boys lined up, staring into the faces of the husky giants from Linden. The Linden players were laughing.

I glanced quickly over my shoulder at the figure wrapped in a blanket. I saw a hand raised up weakly. Then, pressing my lips together in nervous tension, I peered down the field to where all my hopes lay. I felt a weakness in my legs. I would have given anything to be in that formation.

I fastened my eyes on lanky, gawky Rod Duncan. He was playing quarterback.

There was a second of suspense as the players held themselves motionless. The ball snapped from the center to Rod.

Like a clumsy giraffe, he turned and ran back

12

toward his own goal line, over it, and on to the very limit of the end zone.

The crowd let out a roar of laughter. It was going to be funny all right.

Then something unexpected happened!

Rod stopped and wheeled in his track. His right arm whipped back. Straight as a shot the ball soared fifty, sixty, seventy yards down the field. And there, running under the ball at top speed, was Rod Duncan's sprinter friend, Bill Melton.

Bill never had to change pace. Like the trackman he was, he raced toward the Linden goal. Too late, the Linden defensive backs realized what had happened. There was no way they could catch him.

The crowd was stunned into silence. Roark had scored a touchdown on the first play—the first touchdown any Roark team had made in almost three years. And against mighty Linden!

I ran to one of the officials and asked for a time out. Whatever time was allowed after a touchdown, I knew we needed more.

Down near the Roark goal line, the field was strewn with limp figures. Rod Duncan was in a heap in the end zone.

While they were carrying off the hurt players, I faced the regular Roark team. They crowded around me.

"I hope you appreciate what those guys did for

13

you," I said, trying to lift my voice over the roar of the crowd.

I pointed to the blanketed figure in the stand behind us. " 'Iron Vic' is up there. You all know what 'Iron Vic' means, what the 'Iron Vic' tradition used to mean to Roark. Those fellows just showed that it is still alive. Now guys, go out there and show old 'Iron Vic' and Roark what you can do with a six point lead."

The boys turned and filed out onto the field. Not a word was said. But eleven jaws were set, and eleven pairs of padded shoulders hunched over in more than ordinary determination.

As Bull Stephens passed me, I said, "Bull, you're the Captain. For the rest of the game, you've got to be both Captain and Coach. Make it good."

I stayed to watch the conversion for point after touchdown. Then I watched Roark kick off to Linden. The receiver was stopped in his tracks. They made four yards in three tries, then had to punt. Roark received on its own twenty-seven yard line and ran the ball back to midfield.

On the next play, Bull ran the ball straight through the center of the powerful Linden line for twelve beautiful yards. On the next play he went for seventeen yards. I had never seen such silent ferocity as the Roark blockers were displaying.

I knew now what was going to happen. Before

14

I could reach the runway, Roark had its second touchdown.

I hurried to the locker room. My eleven heroes were sprawled all over the place. A doctor was completing his examination of their bruises.

"No one seriously hurt," he said.

I stopped next to Rod Duncan. He was smiling. "I still think it was a crazy idea." He smiled at me. "How is it going up there?"

I held up a finger. The Roark victory yell was being given again. Another Roark touchdown had obviously just been scored.

"That should be number three so far for Roark," I said.

Rod looked at me with a big grin. "Number three for you, I'd say."

"What do you mean, Rod? You're the guys that did it."

"No, I mean number three for you," he insisted.

"Why for me?"

"It figures," he said loudly enough so the other fellows could hear him. "I just think it's time we started calling you number three. You know—'Iron Vic the Third!'"

Bench-Warmer

M. G. OGAN

MY sophomore year at Springville High School I was third-string fullback playing behind Darryl Owens, a senior, and Phil Jordan, a junior. I only played when our coach, Chuck Randolph, didn't want to run up a big score on some hapless opponent.

I'm Vance Richards. My father owns the Richards Construction Company in Springville.

As a sophomore I knew I had some growing to do, weight to gain, and a lot to learn before I'd be first string fullback. We play the single wing formation so the fullback has to run, pass, and kick.

Over the summer I worked on the new courthouse Dad was building over in Cotton Valley. I chose the job of hod carrier to build my leg muscles. When I wasn't working I practiced punting and passing every night with my kid brother, Fuller. He's junior high and wants to be a football player, too.

I'd grown to six feet and weighed 190 pounds when my junior school term opened. But Phil Jordan hadn't been sitting in a deck chair the past summer. Instead he'd gone to a football camp over in Mississippi.

After the first few days of practice I knew I couldn't beat Phil and make the first team. He was an inch shorter than I, but he outweighed me by ten pounds. He could boot the ball consistently 50 yards from the line of scrimmage. He was faster than I am and better in a broken field. And how he could throw that football!

So all right, I reasoned, I'll warm the bench another year, but next year? Watch out.

Coach Randolph used me more than he had last season and I played a full game when Phil pulled a hamstring muscle. I scored twice on line plunges and threw a touchdown pass. But Phil was ready to go next Friday night and I was benched again.

Phil made All State that year. It's no disgrace to play behind someone as good as he was.

My junior year summer was spent working on Dad's construction jobs and practicing with Fuller. I'd finished growing but gained ten pounds and hardened up. I was ready to eclipse Phil Jordan's record that had won the conference championship for Springville High.

Late in August we went up to register for the new school year. Football practice started that afternoon. Ahead of me in line was a husky black, Willie Brown. He was new to our school so I introduced myself.

"My father is an electrician and works for your father now," Willie told me. "I was a freshman at Grambling High School last year."

"Are you coming out for football?"

Willie grimaced. "Man, I don't know. Education comes first my father says. I had to quit frosh football at Grambling when my marks slipped."

"Hey, give it a try," I said. "You get in trouble with your marks and I'll help out. Anyway, almost all of our teachers are football fans. They'll give you extra help if they know you're trying."

Willie looked like a tackle to me. He was built to play football. I wanted him up there blocking when my number was called.

Willie came out for football that afternoon and started working with the awkward squad on the basics of blocking and tackling. Coach Randolph is a bear about basics.

"Trying to play football without knowing the basic elements of the game," he says, "is like trying to multiply without knowing your multiplication tables."

Bud Watson, a second-string tight end last year, was being converted to play fullback behind me. I kicked farther and with more accuracy than

Bud. My passing was better. I was also faster than Bud running the ball.

At the end of the first week of practice I heard Coach Randolph tell one of his assistants, "It's a shame about Willie Brown. He's got potential but we haven't time to give him the individual attention he needs. I'm afraid we'll have to cut him from the squad."

That evening I talked with Coach Randolph in his office. "I persuaded Willie to come out for football," I told him. "I feel responsible for the kid. Can you leave him on the squad another week and let me work with him?"

"You're willing to do that, Vance?" Coach Randolph was surprised.

"I'm willing."

"Then we'll keep Willie another week and see how it goes."

Monday afternoon Willie reported to me down in a corner of the field. I had him do a few wind sprints, timing him with a stopwatch, and was surprised at his speed.

"Do you want to play in the backfield?" I asked. "You're fast enough on your feet."

"I'd sure like that, Vance."

"Okay. That's the way we'll coach you."

I taught him to hit the ball with his toe when he kicked instead of the side of his foot. When Willie had the hang of it he was kicking the ball 60 yards.

Willie learned to grip the ball when throwing

a pass instead of shoveling it off his palm. He got so he could hit my numbers whenever I ran a pass pattern.

Every so often Coach Randolph came down to see how we were making out. He'd watch us for a while but didn't say anything.

I coached Willie about carrying the ball. "The hole you're supposed to hit isn't open sometimes," I told him. "Say you've been called to go between guard and center. That hole's clogged up. That's probably because the tackle has read the play and squeezed in. You cut and run where that tackle isn't."

Willie liked to run carrying the ball in his hand but I broke him of that.

I neglected my homework that week to go to the house Willie's father had rented. Besides helping him with his homework we studied the book of plays. Willie was a quick learner.

"How come you're so anxious to help my boy?" his father asked.

"Because he can be a really good football player," I said. "In three years he may get an athletic scholarship. Who knows what Willie can do after he's had a college education?"

Mr. Brown was a big, slow-moving man. He went to stare out a window. "Yeah, who knows?" I heard him say.

Monday afternoon the next week we played a first team versus second team game. Coach Ran-

20

dolph gave the second team the ball on their twenty.

Willie instead of Bud Watson lined up as their single wing fullback. Right then I was proud to have coached him.

On defense I'm the middle linebacker. "You guys are just as close to our goal as you're going to get," I told the second team.

Willie took the ball on their first play for a slant off our left tackle. Their blocking broke down and Willie should have been stopped cold but he broke two tackles to break into the clear.

Fast? Our cornerback missed him. He was just across the fifty yard line when I blocked him out of bounds.

"That's the way to go." Willie reached down and gave me a hand to my feet. "You okay, Vance?"

"My face is red but otherwise I'm all right."

We held them there and Willie punted into the end zone. We started from our twenty. Willie was their middle linebacker.

We could move the football but Willie seemed to be in on every tackle. Once he blitzed and caught me behind the line of scrimmage.

Coach Randolph and his assistants were in a tight huddle watching the game. They finally substituted Bud for Willie.

Now we could move further and better. Bud tried hard but couldn't match Willie's performance, either on offense or defense.

21

When the game was over I felt good. I was proud of Willie and told him so in the locker room.

"I didn't know what football was all about until you worked with me, Vance," Willie said.

"Maybe my coaching helped," I said, "but you're a born football player."

Our first opponent, Addison High, had a weak team this season. I started the game and scored two touchdowns, one on a 37-yard run. We had them 33-0 before Coach Randolph put in Willie and the second team.

The first play from scrimmage Willie raced 64 yards for a touchdown. He was passing and running for a second score when Coach Randolph put in Bud Watson.

Willie came off the field hurt and scowling. "What did I do wrong, Coach?" he asked.

I'll never forget Coach Randolph's answer. "You did everything right at the wrong time, Willie. We're trying to keep the score down."

He gave his head a thoughtful shake when Willie came over to join me on the bench.

I tried to say the right things to Willie about the way he'd played but the words stuck in my throat. I had experience going for me but Willie was a better player as a sophomore than I was as a senior.

I wished I'd let Coach Randolph cut him from the squad. Sooner or later Willie would have me warming the bench again this season.

I played the first half of the next game; Willie played the second half. We won 23-7. But he'd gained more ground than I had and completed three passes to my two. The following game Willie started; I played the second half. We won again, 34-14. I scored one. Willie scored twice. His second touchdown was running back the kickoff 97 yards. That run broke the game open for us.

By this time Willie and I were just nodding to each other when we shared a class or passed in the hall. This wasn't Willie's fault. I was the sorehead.

The next game Willie started and I didn't get in until late in the fourth quarter. It was the game after that when the bottom fell out of the bucket.

We were playing a strong team, Central High. No one had beaten them yet and we were still undefeated. It was Willie who started at fullback.

Without my realizing it the first team was split down the middle. Half thought Willie should be a starter because I wasn't quite as good as he was. The other half reasoned I was a senior and had worked hard for a slot on the first team. Willie had three years of competition ahead of him. Why shouldn't Vance Richards be playing?

In the middle of the first quarter one or two players missed key blocks. Willie was smeared for a loss. When he tried to pass his protection broke down and he was sacked three times.

Now this looked one way from the stands. The fans thought Willie wasn't trying. It looked another way from the bench. The team was letting him down.

Twice during that first half we were penalized for taking too much time in the huddle. The players were bickering with each other.

We were lucky to come out of that first half with a 0-0 ball game.

The team was still growling at each other. Coach Randolph stopped that with two words, "Shut up!"

Crossing his arms on his chest he stared at us. Now Coach Randolph is usually a low-key guy. He doesn't bluster and shout.

"If someone had told me this would happen to one of my teams I wouldn't have believed it," he said in a sarcastic, cutting voice. "Did I say team? You guys aren't a team any longer. You're a bunch of silly school kids making yourself look like fools. I'm ashamed I have to send you out to play another half. Now hear this, you starters. I'm giving you just two minutes of this second half to play like a team. If you don't shape up I'm yanking all of you and we'll let the second team lose this one for us."

The first team took Coach Randolph at his word. Nobody missed their blocks now. Willie got the running room he needed and slashed across for two touchdowns.

I played the fourth quarter. They scored on us and ran the ball over to make it 14-8. We were on the defensive most of the time. While they were driving for a second touchdown I read a pass play right and went up with the receiver to come down with the ball.

That was on our 14-yard line.

We started back up the field and were across the 50 when the gun sounded ending the game. We should have made better progress. My interference wasn't forming fast enough when I got the ball.

Guards were slow pulling out of the line when we ran the power sweep.

I believe every back has a touch of paranoia now and then. We feel we're not getting the co-operation we need from the rest of the team. I know I went off the field at the end of that game sore at some of my teammates. Which should have told me how Willie felt in the first half when they let him down but it didn't.

Monday morning I have study hall first period. Coach Randolph sent for me. "Sit down, Vance," he said when I reached his office under the stadium. "I have a problem I want to discuss with you."

"Yes, sir?"

"I've talked with the vocational counselor. He says you want to take Engineering in college. Is that right?"

"Yes, sir, it is." This conversation puzzled me. "You mentioned a problem, Coach."

"We'll get to that. First I want to congratulate you. Willie Brown would be off the squad if it hadn't been for the time and trouble you took to coach him."

"Maybe I made a mistake," I said.

"Do you mean that?"

"No, sir, I don't."

Willie Brown knocked and came into the office. He glanced at me. "Do you want to see me now?"

"Yes, Willie. Sit down over there beside Vance." Coach Randolph regarded us thoughtfully. "I've told Vance we have a problem, Willie. I want you two fellows to solve it for me."

"Make Vance a starter," Willie said, "and your problem is solved. I'm only a sophomore. I can play behind him for a year."

There was no bitterness in the way he spoke. "I wouldn't be anywhere if it wasn't for Vance coaching me. I know that and so does the rest of the team."

"My job as coach is to field the best eleven players I have," Coach Randolph said. "Vance, you're too good to be warming the bench. You are, too, Willie. So both of you will be in the starting backfield this coming game. Willie, you'll stay at fullback. Vance, you'll be right halfback. Now I'm going to leave it up to you two to pull the team together."

"Just how do we do that?" Willie asked while we were walking back to classes. "This is a big one coming up."

We faced another undefeated team Friday

26

night, Holly Grove, and we were a one-touchdown underdog.

"Leave that to me, Willie," I said. "I've got an idea."

I worked hard that week on the halfback's blocking and running assignments. After practice Thursday Coach Randolph named me captain for the Holly Grove game.

Suiting up the next evening I asked Coach Randolph if I could have a word with the team alone before the kick-off.

He cocked his head, thought about it, then said, "All right, Vance."

Coach Randolph and his assistants left me alone with the first team a minute before we would take the field.

I went over to Willie and made him stand up.

"Any of you guys who miss a block or do anything else to make this fellow look bad is going to eat his teeth after I catch up with him after tonight's game. You let me down and you'll have Willie to settle with. Isn't that right?"

"That's right," Willie said.

"Now let's go out and play football," I told the team.

Holly Grove was as fast, big, and tough as they were rated. We stopped them twice within our own ten that first half.

But even the best team when you keep them out of your end zone twice begins to wonder.

When we had the ball, coming up to the huddle, I asked Willie, "Do you feel like throwing a bomb?"

Willie grinned. "Never felt more like it."

I told the quarterback what play to call. He stared at me as if I was out of my mind but called the play.

Willie would have to pass from the end zone. I had to fake the cornerback, get two steps on him, and take the pass running.

But the whole play depended on Willie's protection. He got it and threw.

The cornerback evidently didn't think we were crazy enough to throw from our own end zone so shaking him was no problem. I turned my head and there was the ball. Catching it over my shoulder I tucked it away and went in standing up.

That was the beginning of the end for Holly Grove. I tossed some halfback passes for completions; Willie threw five, four complete. We ran off tackle and up the middle. By halftime we had them 35-0.

It was a real team effort.

"I'm proud of you tonight," Coach Randolph said during the intermission. "Keep it up and we'll win the conference title."

We kept it up and whipped Holly Grove 54-7.

There was no stopping Springville after that game. Willie and I would sometimes switch positions in the backfield. The other team never knew what was coming next.

28

Willie and I studied together again to keep his and my marks up.

Both of us made All State after Springville won the conference.

After we'd won our final game Coach Randolph wanted to see me.

"You may think you want to be an engineer," he said, "but I think you should be a coach. Do some thinking about it, will you, Vance?"

I did think about it. I talked it over with my father. I'm playing for Louisiana Tech in Ruston now, as a quarterback, and studying to be a coach.

The Fullback from Liechtenstein

JACK RITCHIE

NONE of us thought it was much of a trade.

I mean we're all in favor of "cultural exchange," or whatever you want to call it, but there was Tank O'Brien going to one of those European Gymnasiums—that's what they call high school over there—and here we are stuck with this kid in *lederhosen*.

Mostly we blamed Principal Walker for what happened. It's a fact that Tank O'Brien was in the upper ten percent of his class and maybe he *was* a good specimen to send over there to show the Europeans whàt we look like—sort of pretend that Tank is just an average American and give them an inferiority complex—but the hard part to take is that Tank is All Fox Valley Conference Fullback and he was just a sophomore when he got the honor last year.

Tank is practically the team. He *is* the team.

I think that Tank's mistake was getting A's in German.

Why didn't Mr. Walker send somebody like Jerry Gilman? He's a good enough halfback, except that he's a little tackle shy. He stops running when he knows he's going to be hit and sometimes you sure could use a few extra yards.

Or Billy Beneke? He's the left end. Can do the hundred in ten seconds flat and has good hands for a pass—but only when the ball comes over his right shoulder. Don't know what it is, but when it floats to him over the left shoulder, he just can't hang on to it.

Or even me? I'm the second-string fullback and I usually get in the game the last five minutes when we're two or three touchdowns ahead and O'Brien needs the rest.

But they shipped Tank O'Brien to Europe.

The way the exchange thing works is that we send one of our students over there for a year, and we get one of theirs while he's gone.

Heinrich Fronmholz is his name.

Anyway he came from Liechtenstein. That's just about the smallest country over there and they got a Prince and a Princess and they're always neutral when anything happens.

Mr. Walker introduced Heinrich to the whole school in assembly the first day of the semester. He was wearing the *lederhosen,* Heinrich was. They're short leather pants and the girls thought that was cute—but then you know girls. I expected him to yodel any minute, but he just made a little speech saying how everybody was so nice to him since he came over—especially Mr. and Mrs. O'Brien, because that was who he was staying with.

And so Heinrich is in school and he calls all the girls "Miss" when he talks to them and they sort of sigh. Once he said *Fraulein* to Barbara Higgins and she got glassy-eyed and dropped her books. If he could sing, I don't know what would happen.

Well, we could take all that, but what happened was that Heinrich showed up for football practice. In those short pants.

At first I thought he was just going to watch, but he went over to Coach Benson and said, "Sir, if it is permissible, may I participate?"

He wanted to play football, that's what it was.

Coach Benson rubbed his neck and thought that over. "Have you ever played football?"

"Yes, sir," Heinrich said. "I was chiefly Center Forward, but at times I have played Inside Right Forward."

Jerry Gilman opened his big fat mouth. "He means soccer, coach. That's what they call football in Europe."

Coach Benson glared at Jerry. "I am acquainted with the game," he snapped.

"Well, Heinrich," he said and patted him on

32

the shoulder. "I'm afraid that we play the game a little differently over here. A lot rougher."

"Sir," Heinrich said, "I'm ready to adjust. I will do my utmost."

Coach just looked Heinrich over, especially the short pants, and sighed. "All right, Heinrich, get into a uniform. Gilman, you go with him and show him how to put on the gear. And tell him a few things about football."

We were all set to make the best of the situation, but when Gilman and Heinrich came jogging back upfield, there was Heinrich wearing number thirty-three.

Thirty-three! That was O'Brien's number.

We all stared, including Coach Benson, and Gilman shrugged. "I couldn't help it. That was the only uniform that fit."

Looking Heinrich over, it suddenly struck me that Heinrich was pretty big at that. Those short pants and bare knees had us fooled.

Coach Benson put the ball on the fifty-yard line. "All right, Heinrich, you're the fullback on the B team. We'll let you handle the ball a few times. Just so you get the feel of things."

The quarterback shoveled the ball to Heinrich on the first play from scrimmage, and we all came charging in.

And I mean *all*.

Not just the line, but the whole backfield.

Maybe that wasn't football, but here was Hein-

33

rich wearing O'Brien's thirty-three, and we just saw red about that.

About five of us got to Heinrich and the other six had to be disappointed. But after all there was just so much to Heinrich, and we'd have to wait our turn next time—if Heinrich ever carried the ball again.

When the pack was peeled off, Heinrich didn't have the ball. I did.

He looked at it in my hands and then apologized to his teammates. "I am sorry, but it is indeed difficult to retain, is it not, when one is pummeled?"

He fumbled, that's what he meant.

On our first down, we went into punt formation. That wasn't football either, but we wanted Heinrich to get his hands on the ball again and we wanted to get our hands on Heinrich.

The B team quarterback cooperated by sending Heinrich back to receive.

I did the kicking. I'm not as good as O'Brien—nobody is—but this time I got leg behind the ball and sent out a high floater. It went to Heinrich on the five.

I guess he should have called for a fair catch, but maybe he didn't know what that was. Anyway, we were all there when the ball came down.

Heinrich held on to it, but not for long. After three or four tackles it squirted out of his hands and into the end zone. Barrows, our right tackle, fell on it for six points.

34

We made the extra point and then I kicked off to the B team. It seemed like one of the best kicks of my life—usually I can't get within fifteen yards of the kind of kick that O'Brien puts out. The ball went into the end zone, and the B team took over on its own twenty.

Heinrich got the ball handed to him for the next three downs. He didn't fumble—I'll give him credit for that—even with the way we mowed him down. The first time he carried, he lost eight yards. The second time, seven. The third, four.

When Heinrich got up after that, he slowly looked over the members of the B team and spoke. "Gentlemen, I think that perhaps I could do better for the team if you detained the opposition a few moments longer. No? That would give me sufficient opportunity to develop momentum."

He wasn't getting any blocking. That's what he meant. Not enough time to work up a head of steam. His line was leaking like a sieve.

A few of Heinrich's linemen blushed. They'd been stepping aside and letting us through for a crack at Heinrich.

His eyes went over them again. "It is fourth down, is it not? We are on our one-yard line? Is it usual to kick in a situation such as this?"

Byron, the second-string quarterback, grinned. "We do that sometimes."

Heinrich nodded solemnly. "Shall I assist in protecting the kicker?"

"No," Byron said. "We'll let you do the kicking. It's a big honor."

We all looked at each other and I guess we came to an agreement. No rushing. Let him get the kick off. Just for laughs.

I drifted back to the forty with Gilman.

The ball went to Heinrich in the rear of the end zone. He took the step and put a leg to the ball. It was a real *thunk!*

I listened to that and I was still thinking about it when I noticed that I wasn't going to have to run *in* for the ball. It was floating up there—pretty, if you like those things—and it came to me as a shock that it was going over my head. Way over. On top of everything else, it got the lucky bounces and cartwheeled away from me. When I finally picked it up, I was back on my own thirty.

I mulled that over as I started the run-back. Heinrich had kicked from deep in his end zone . . . there was the happy bounce, of course . . . but still, the ball had traveled about . . .

I was adding up the figures when the express train hit me.

I've been tackled by almost everybody on the squad in scrimmage at one time or another, but I can just about tell who it is by the feel of the contact.

I lay there, tasting the sod and listening to the buzzing in my head, and finally came to a conclusion. O'Brien must have got me. He took a jet back from Europe, jumped into a suit, and . . .

36

The coach's voice came to me worried and from out of the foggy distance. "Are you all right, Taylor?"

"Sure," I mumbled automatically. I looked up at the blur of faces. "I must have stumbled over something."

"Heinrich tackled you," Jerry Gilman said, and he sounded awed. "You fumbled and B team recovered."

Things began clicking back into focus, and I could make out Heinrich.

"You were inattentive," he said. "And that accounts for your present reclining position and the loss of the ball. The impact came as a surprise to you."

I was still thinking about that kick when I got hit. That's what he meant.

I got to my feet with some help. "I'm fine."

The coach didn't think so. "You'd better go to the bench for a while. I'll put Sawicki in for you."

And so I sat and watched.

Heinrich's kick and his tackle must have done something for the B team. Pulled it together. There was blocking.

Regan took the ball the first two times and got a total of eight yards.

And then the pigskin went to Heinrich.

The line made a nice hole for him, and he barreled through like he was looking for water after a day in the desert. Manley had a shot at

37

him and missed. So did Sawicki. And then Heinrich was in the clear and Gilman was chasing him.

I waited for the tackle. After all, Gilman could do the hundred in. . . .

Heinrich was pulling away when he crossed the goal line.

That's the way it went.

They quit when it was too dark to see the ball and by then the score was 24 to 7, in favor of the B team. Heinrich scored three touchdowns, kicked the extra points, and frosted the cake with a thirty-five yard field goal.

I began to wonder if maybe Liechtenstein sent Heinrich over just to make *us* feel inferior.

Coach Benson might have made up his mind right then, but he waited until the end of the week before he put me on the second team and Heinrich took my place. I'd been expecting that, but it still did rub me a little.

Heinrich didn't wear those short pants to classes after the first week. I guess that was the only improvement—in anything.

I got a letter from O'Brien the next week. Everything was fine with *him*. He was playing soccer and was outside left forward or something like that.

Our first game was with River Falls High and we took that one 32 to 7. I played the last seven minutes and didn't do anything in particular for Stevenson High. The team—I mean Heinrich—

downed Dawson the next week, 21 to 0, and Rufus Tech the week after, 33 to 14.

Heinrich didn't score *all* the points. Gilman took a pass from over his good shoulder in the Tech game and carried it into the end zone. I kicked the extra point. Big deal.

It seemed to me that just about everybody on the team forgot about O'Brien. But I didn't. We were buddies. Even if he was over there in short pants and kicking a basketball all over some bunch of grass.

I was walking home from practice one afternoon and thinking that football wasn't much of a game anyway and also considering that maybe I ought to switch my language course from German to Spanish, when Heinrich fell into step beside me.

"I regret most sincerely that I have displaced you, Taylor," he said. "Had I known this would occur I do not believe I would have entered into football at all."

I managed a shrug. "That's the way it goes."

"You are not angry with me? I mean that you do not seem to seek any conversation."

I shrugged again. "Just got nothing to say." I glanced at him. "Why aren't you wearing the leather shorts? Everybody thinks they're cute."

"I wore them the first week only to please Mr. Walker and Mrs. O'Brien who desired that I be picturesque. I have a preference for long trousers. Even in Liechtenstein."

We walked a half a block without any talk and then he said, "I have heard much of this O'Brien."

"Best guy in the world," I said. "He could do anything."

"Ah? He is a god?"

I scowled. What did he mean by that?

But Heinrich smiled. "Is O'Brien taller than you are?"

I thought about it. "Well, no. I'm about an inch taller."

"Ah," Heinrich said. "But then he weighs more than you do?"

"No. I weigh about ten pounds more."

"Then he is fleeter of foot?"

"No," I snapped. "He is not fleeter of. . . ." And then I remembered. "Sure. He's faster."

Heinrich still smiled. "Perhaps when you *compete* with him? No? And yet I have learned that when you run alone you can be two-tenths of a second faster in the hundred-yard dash than he can. It is in the records of Coach Benson."

"Now, look," I said. "Just what are you getting at?"

His face was thoughtful. "You are bigger than O'Brien, you are faster than O'Brien, and yet you were on the second team and he was on the first?"

I felt myself flushing. "We can't *all* be on the first team."

He nodded. "True. Still. . . ." He walked a few yards and then sighed. "I have written to O'Brien

40

about our games, and he has written to me. He is very disappointed."

That was hard to believe. "Disappointed? But we won all our games so far."

Heinrich's smile returned. "A correction, please. *We* did not win the games. *I* did."

I stared at him. "There are *ten* other men on the team—in case you didn't notice."

He shrugged. "Their presence is required by the rules of the game, of course. One cannot say much more. But in actuality, *I* am the team, just as O'Brien was the team when he was here. He had hoped that perhaps things might change while he was gone, but unfortunately not. He and I still deal with the same inferior material."

I was going to slug him right then and there, but he held up a hand. "There is no need for anger. One can not fight with the truth." And then he turned the corner and walked toward the O'Brien house.

When I got home, I didn't eat supper. Who can eat when you feel the way I did? My mother got worried about that and was all ready to call a doctor, so finally at nine I ate a few sandwiches just to stop that.

Our schedule called for us to meet Parkview East that afternoon on our own field. Parkview wasn't the strongest team in the league, but still could be dangerous. It had a 1-and-2 record.

The squad reported to the locker room under

the stadium an hour before game time and we began suiting up.

After a while Coach Benson frowned. "Where's Heinrich?"

Nobody seemed to know, and the coach started working hard on his chewing gum.

He stewed for about twenty minutes and then left the room. When he came back he still looked worried, but not so much. "I just phoned. Mr. O'Brien took Heinrich to Clover Falls last night to see some of the O'Brien relatives and they stayed over night. They got a late start back this morning, and Heinrich will be a little late for the game." He turned to me. "Taylor, you're starting at fullback."

My hands got clammy. "Me? Starting?"

"That's right. Just do your best until Heinrich comes."

My voice squeaked. "But I never *started* before. I always got in the last five minutes or so."

"Well, you start now," he said irritably. "You're all we got." He turned to the rest of the team. "Just hold out—do your best—until Heinrich gets here."

When we trotted out onto the field, I think everybody felt just the same as I did. Scared. We'd always had O'Brien before. Or Heinrich. But now there was just *us*.

We won the toss and naturally elected to receive. The kickoff came to Jerry Gilman on our seventeen and he carried to the twenty-five. He

42

might have picked up another five or so, but when the tacklers converged, he stopped and braced himself for the contact.

On the first play from scrimmage, I took the ball. I tried to bull my way through a small hole, but I got hit hard and the ball slewed out of my hands. Parkview East recovered.

When I got to my feet, I knew what everybody was thinking. Heinrich wouldn't have fumbled.

It took Parkview only five plays before the halfback skirted into the end zone for the TD. The point after was missed and that left the score at 6 to 0.

Gilman took the kick again and brought the ball back to our twenty-nine. I picked up two yards on the first play, and Collier, the left half, three on the next. On third down, Sawicki faded back for a long pass. Beneke was in the clear a couple of yards beyond his defenseman, and the spiral was a beauty. There was only one trouble. The ball was coming to Beneke over his left shoulder. We could all see that's the way it was going to be, and we waited for him to drop the ball. He did.

We punted on fourth down and Parkview brought the ball back to its thirty-two. Seven plays later the score was 13 to 0.

It went like that. Nothing right for us and almost everything right for Parkview. Where in the world was Heinrich?

With two minutes left to play in the half, the score stood at 26 to 0 and Parkview had the ball on our six-yard line all ready to add another six or seven points and there were four downs to do it.

We lined up for our goal-line stand—if you want to call it that—we knew that Parkview was going to score anyway—when we noticed some activity on the sidelines. Somebody handed Coach Benson a note, he grinned and trotted down the ramp to the dressing room.

Instinctively we all knew what had happened. Heinrich was back and suiting up.

We grinned at each other and the tiredness left our bones.

Jerry Gilman pounded a fist into his palm. "All right, let's not make it any tougher for Heinrich than we have to. Hold that line."

And we did.

Parkview East lost the ball on downs on our four, and our first play ran out the clock.

Trotting back to the dressing room, we were happy as a bunch of kids, slapping backs and punching and all that stuff. Even me. Heinrich was back and the second half was going to be another story. What difference did 26 to 0 make anyway? Heinrich could make that up and more.

Heinrich was waiting for us in the dressing room.

There was only one thing wrong.

He leaned on a crutch, and his left foot was

44

swathed in a bandage. He smiled weakly. "An unfortunate automobile accident."

And so we sat down on the benches and we looked at the cement floor, and we were silent. 26 to 0. What would the score be by the end of the game? 50, 60, or 70 to 0?

Heinrich spoke. "Coach Benson, is it not possible at this point to concede the game to the opponent? After all, it is apparent that what remains will be a . . . how do you say . . . a slaughter?"

Coach Benson said nothing. He didn't even look up.

"We must face facts," Heinrich said. "I am unable to play. The leader is gone and therefore defeat is inevitable."

I shifted uncomfortably on the bench and I noticed that a few of the others did too.

Heinrich went on. "Without a leader they are nothing, Coach Benson. They are ridden by fears and complexes." He stood up. His eyes settled on Jerry Gilman. "For instance, you, Jerry, have this fear of being tackled. Fear, of course, is nothing to be ashamed of." He smiled thinly. "But does it not seem more logical that *anyone* who is afraid of being tackled does not *belong* on a football team?"

Jerry Gilman went white and looked like a bulldog ready to bite.

Heinrich held up a hand. "Please do not be angry. I have not for one moment suggested cow-

45

ardice. I am aware that two years ago when you were a sophomore you were tackled and you fumbled. Because of this fumble the team lost the game and the championship. You have never forgotten that and you are determined *never* again to fumble, even if it costs you five yards every time you carry the ball." Heinrich smiled again. "This desire to protect the ball—this intense wish never to take a chance—this is not cowardice, is it?"

Before Gilman could say something, Heinrich turned to Beneke. "And you, Beneke, cannot catch a pass which comes over your left shoulder. This reduces your efficiency—your value to the team—by at least fifty percent. Perhaps more, since all your opponents are well aware of this fact.

"Beneke, I understand that when you were a freshman, you were pursuing a pass—a pass which was coming over your left shoulder—when you stepped on a kickoff tee someone had carelessly left on the field and broke your ankle. And since then your mind has become conditioned, has it not? When a pass comes to you from the left, you think deep within you that you are about to stumble again and break your ankle? And so with this preoccupation you drop the ball?"

Beneke blinked and it seemed as though he were looking at something for the first time.

"A mental block," Heinrich said. "This is something difficult to overcome. One requires intelligence, understanding, courage. In your case, Beneke, I'm afraid that. . . ." Heinrich sighed.

And then he went over the squad and he had something to say about almost everybody.

We all knew what he was doing. We've listened to fight talks before. But this was . . . well . . . different. Not quite fair. He was touching where it hurt.

He saved me for last.

"In your case, Taylor," he said. "We come to one who lacks confidence completely."

Confidence? What did he mean by that? I had as much confidence as anybody.

He read my mind and shook his head. "*No* confidence, Taylor, and I think that you are actually *afraid* to excel."

Heinrich was way off. Where did he get something screwy like that?

"You have a brother," Heinrich said. "I am told that he is at present at a university and that he is magnificent at fullback. This you no doubt take pride in. He was also most excellent in this high school when he attended, and he is the possessor of several records."

That part was right enough. My brother was about the best back ever to play on a Stevenson squad.

"But the most important point of all," Heinrich said. "Is that he is *four* years older than you are. And being four years older, he was bigger than you are, he could kick farther, he could run faster.

47

He was there ahead of you all the time and you could never catch up—no matter how you tried —because of this four-year difference. And while you were frustrated by this, your mind eventually told itself that you would *never* catch up and that you must *adjust* to this. An adjustment such as this is in a sense admirable, but there should be a limit upon it. It should not continue forever. However you have chosen always to see *another* brother ahead of you and always unsurpassable— a brother whose name might be Taylor or perhaps O'Brien or even Heinrich Fronmholz."

His voice became more pointed. "You engage in—how shall we say—hero worship? It is fine to admire those of remarkable capabilities, but one must not do so to the injury of one's own potentialities. And in time too, I think that you became *afraid* to excel even when you could, because your brother—this Taylor, this O'Brien, or even this Heinrich Fronmholz—might not *like* you if you did."

He shook his head sadly. "But one must grow up. One must not continue to buy friendships by such concessions."

Where did he get all this crazy stuff? But my face was red, and I was sweating.

I think that by now we all wanted to lynch Heinrich, but somehow we just didn't seem to have the energy. We just sat there and, I guess, we each had something to think about.

I don't know how long we would have kept

that up, but one of the officials knocked on the door and wanted to know if we were going to play any more football. Everybody else was on the field and had been waiting for ten minutes.

We walked out there. I mean *walked*. No jogging and running. And we were quiet. Maybe everybody else was still thinking—like I was.

I took a couple of deep breaths of the cool air and that cleared my head. Really cleared it.

I kicked off to Parkview East. The stride was just right, and the sound was just right. That ball was going somewhere.

The Parkview receivers watched it go over their heads and right over the goal-post crossbars. Parkview took over on its own twenty yard line.

I thought about that kick as the defense went in, and maybe everybody else on the team did too. My brother held the league record for a field goal—officially forty-nine yards, but when you add the ten extra yards to the goal post in the end zone, that made it fifty-nine. And the best O'Brien had ever done had been against Tech last year from the Tech forty-two. My kick wasn't a field goal—as far as the records counted—but still I had kicked from my own forty and that made it. . . .

Three plays later, Parkview hadn't been able to move the ball more than three yards and went into punt formation.

Jerry Gilman gathered it on our forty-five and took it along the side lines. At their forty-five, three Parkview tacklers converged on Gilman and I thought the play would end there. But this time Gilman didn't stop and let himself be tackled.

He hesitated only a fraction of a second and then picked up a burst of speed. Two of the tacklers had a shot at him and missed, and the third was taken off his feet. Gilman went all the way, and we got the point after. That made it 26 to 7.

We held on defense and when we got the ball, we marched down the field with a series of running plays. I went off left tackle for the last eight yards to make it 26 to 14, and that was the score at the end of the third quarter.

Parkview stiffened in the fourth and held us on its twenty-four. I tried for the field goal and made it. No record kick, but the ball went high over the crossbars and into the crowd. 26 to 17.

The next five minutes were rough for all of us. Parkview dug in and was hoping to preserve the upset. But with four minutes left and our ball, I found a big hole waiting for me and stormed through. I carried all the way from our thirty-six, and nobody was near me when I crossed the goal line. With the point after, that made it 26 to 24, still Parkview.

Parkview let the kickoff bounce into the end zone and took over on its twenty. With less than four minutes left to play, Parkview tried to run out the clock but was forced to punt on fourth down.

50

Gilman picked up the punt and carried it back to the Parkview twenty-nine before he got nailed.

We called time out and went into a huddle. There were less than fifteen seconds left.

"Not much sense in trying anything but a field goal," Gilman said. "All we need is three points. Think you can do it, Taylor?"

I straightened up and looked at the goal posts. Yes, I could make it. I knew that deep inside of me. Today I could make that kick ten times out of ten. Twenty times out of twenty.

But my mind went to something else. Winning the game was important but there were other things important too.

"I think we ought to try 27-A," I said.

It took them a while to remember what that was. It was a play Coach Benson had dreamed up, but one we had never used in a game.

Because we couldn't.

The play calls for the quarterback to fade with the ball and then flip to me wide to the left and still behind the line of scrimmage. In the meantime Beneke cuts from left end to right side of the field. I throw the pass and he takes it over his *left* shoulder.

Beneke got white. "Now wait a minute, Taylor. All we need is three points. We don't have to go for the touchdown. You ought to be able to make the kick."

51

"I don't know about that," I said rubbing my chin. "I don't think so."

Beneke appealed to the rest of the squad. "But all of you know I can't catch a pass over my left shoulder."

I'm not the quarterback, but I'm the team captain when I play. My word carries some weight.

But more than that, everybody on the squad knew what I was trying to do and I could see that everyone agreed with me.

Beneke might have tried to argue his way out of the play, but we snapped out of the huddle and took our positions. There was nothing for him to do but take his place in the line.

The quarterback took the ball into our backfield and tossed to me. There was nobody in front of me and I think I could have carried it all the way, but I waited and watched Beneke.

He made his diagonal and sped toward the spot. I cocked my arm and threw.

When Beneke looked back his face was still white. He reached the point, and the ball floated over his left shoulder and into his arms.

This time he held on to it and sprinted into the end zone.

I made the point after, but that didn't matter. We won 31 to 27.

We stormed back into the dressing room and gave Heinrich a good rough time, slapping him on the back and carrying him around and acting as though he'd won the game.

And I guess he had.

When he calmed down a little, Heinrich still grinned and *walked* to a bench. He sat down and began unwinding the bandages from his foot.

We stared at him and the room got quiet.

Heinrich looked up and it seemed like his eyes laughed. "I did not say that I had been *injured* in the accident. You merely leaped to this conclusion because I had a bandage on my foot."

The bandage came off and he put on his shoe. "It is true there was an accident—a mild scraping of fenders with Mr. O'Brien's car and another. But this gave me an idea."

His face became sober. "Actually I arrived five minutes after the game started but I remained in the stands and watched you play. What I saw was a dispirited team—a team which depended upon *one* man to *save* it. I did not like this. It is not good for you. It is not good for me. And so I decided that I would not play at all. I came down here and put the bandage on my foot. It would be better if you lost without me than won with me. And to this I think you will agree. Especially now."

Coach Benson had two first-string fullbacks the rest of the season. Heinrich and me.

When O'Brien comes back next year, I think he might have a hard time getting the fullback job away from me.

But I'll never find out for sure. I won't be here.

I've been getting A's in German lately, and when Heinrich goes back to Liechtenstein, I'll be going with him. Mr. Walker picked me as the exchange student for next year. Heinrich is going on to college to get his degree in psychology.

I wonder what this soccer is all about.

Dark, Dank and Dismal

WADE H. MOSBY

AT the start of the season the sportswriters were having their usual ball about what a terrific team we were going to have at Colton Tech.

From last year, we had halfbacks George Darkner and Vlad Dankowicz. George Abbis was a letterman at quarterback, and I figured to do as well as any at fullback. Maybe you remember me —Kevin O'Brien—from last year's third team?

Anyway, our line wasn't too bad, and against the second stringers it could open holes big enough to stampede elephants through. Sideways. After the first week of practice, the whole campus was buzzing that this was the year we were going to beat State.

Well, we were as surprised as anyone when Melton College and Seminary beat us, 7 to 0. The next week Crandon College won by a touchdown, and Abbis got a leg fracture that put him out of action for the rest of the season.

After the first game, someone had started calling the backfield "Dark, Dank, and Abbismal," but with Abbis out, they changed it. That's how I got my nickname, "Dismal" O'Brien.

Our big trouble, we had learned, was lack of depth. The reason we ripped through the second team so easily was not our speed, elusiveness and talent, as the sportswriters had been saying, but the scrubs' ineptness, sincere desire to avoid collision and complete lack of guile. Which meant that every time we ran in a substitute, it was like putting out a welcome mat with directions to our goal.

Curly Balducci, the coach, got to talking to himself, and what words he had left over for the rest of the world weren't exactly reserved for summit conferences.

On Tuesday night after the Crandon game, we were trying to adapt our defense to some Institute plays our scouts had brought in. We did fairly well, but got caught flat-footed on a quick kick. It was a dandy. Went spiraling right off the field and came down just aft of the slide trombones over where the marching band was practicing. This naturally disrupted marching a bit. Coach ran over to the sidelines.

"All right," he hollered in that sarcastic way of his. "This isn't the Polo Grounds and you don't get to keep fly balls hit into the stands. Now throw it here!"

Some guy in the middle of the band picked up the ball and gave it a flip. I'm still not sure I believe what happened next. That ball didn't get much more than 10 feet of altitude at best, but it didn't seem to need any more than that. It came blistering along as if it had a mind of its own.

Balducci was standing there with his hands on his hips, probably trying to think of something else to holler at the band, when the ball caught him right between the eyes. He sat down. Hard.

A couple of us helped him to his feet. Coach turned to Aqua Watt, the manager. "Aqua," he said in a trembly voice. "I want the guy who threw that ball. Dismal, you be there, too. My office in ten minutes. That's all for the rest of you for tonight."

Well, I could see that he might want to chew out the chucklehead who fired the bean ball, but I couldn't think of any reason why he should be sore at me. Anyway, I showered and dressed in a hurry and got up to Balducci's office in about eight minutes. Aqua Watt was already there with this guy in the band uniform.

"You can go, Aqua," coach said. And Aqua did. "Sit down," coach said to the band guy, and he did. "What's your name?"

"Knocklemeier, sir," said this kid. "Philip A." He was about 5 foot 9, and probably didn't weigh 160 wearing a French horn.

57

"What course are you taking?"

"Music, sir. And sociology. Sir, I'm sorry I hit you. The light was a little bad or I guess you would have caught the ball."

"Never mind that," coach said. "What do you play in the band?"

"The glockenspiel, sir."

"The . . . ah, yes," coach said. "Well, Glockenmeier, I want you to do something for me."

"Knocklemeier, sir. Philip A."

"Oh, sure. Well, Knockle . . . , ah, Phil. I want to see you toss a football a few times."

So that's where I came in. Knocklemeier, Coach and I went down to one end of the field, and Coach had Knocklemeier toss passes to me. The guy was uncanny. He seemed to use no more effort than a guy swatting a fly, but those passes of his would come steaming to me no matter where I was. If it was in the flat, I'd run a few steps, turn and there it was. Same thing for longs, shorts or you name it. You didn't have to split a spleen reaching, either. All you had to do was defend yourself, because if you didn't catch the ball, it would hit you on the head nine times out of ten.

"That's enough," coach said finally. "Knucklespiel, I want you to suit up for practice tomorrow night."

"Knocklemeier, sir," the kid said. "I'd like to, sir, but I'll be busy tomorrow night."

"Busy doing what?"

"It's the last band practice before the Institute game, sir," said Knocklemeier. "Director Billingsley is counting on me. This is the first year he's had a glockenspiel in the marching band, and we have worked out a few numbers for the halftime show."

Coach's chin dropped and he stared at Knocklemeier as if he were a subversive that had just popped up with the toadstools. In a minute he got a grip on himself.

"I'll speak to Billingsley about practicing your number early. Report here at 4:30."

"Yes, sir."

The next night we just ran through signals in preparation for the Institute game. Knocklemeier looked sort of clumsy in a suit, but he tossed a few more passes for Coach, and he could kill ducks with that football.

I walked home with him—he lived near the Delta Gam house—and found out that he came from a little town where they played six man football. They played the game for fun, and put a lot of passing and razzle dazzle into it.

Phil was a sophomore. He hadn't gone out for football at Colton because he wanted to concentrate on his music. He didn't think he'd like the eleven man game, anyway.

"You spend a couple of hours out here every night, and you're too tired to study," he said.

I thought about it that night.

59

Knocklemeier suited up for the Institute game, but coach didn't put him in. He let him change into his band uniform in plenty of time to play the glockenspiel at the half, and you'd think that he had scored four touchdowns, he was that happy. He came back to the locker room with his glockenspiel, which was a sort of one lung xylophone, and knocked off a few numbers for us. We needed cheering up, because Institute had scored and we hadn't.

But Knocklemeier seemed so interested in his music and so unconcerned about the score that the rest of us realized that the world wasn't coming to an end. I'm not saying that this was responsible, but we relaxed in the second half and scored three times. Institute didn't gain more than 20 yards the entire half.

Knocklemeier reported for football practice Monday with a long face. He told Coach that the glockenspiel number had been dropped from the marching band. I saw Balducci look a little guilty, but Knocklemeier didn't suspect anything, and started learning to block, run and tackle with the same intensity I imagined he had given to his music.

That was the worst week of the fall. Balducci drove us until we could hardly get off the field. I expected the kid to break in half, but he was as wiry as a fraternity sofa. By the time we left for Wilson college Friday night, he knew what was expected of the quarterback. Balducci had

60

poured the pass plays into him, and he was familiar with our basic running game.

Wilson was supposed to be the weak sister of the conference, but with the home fans hollering their heads off on that Saturday afternoon, the Wilsons fought like a pack of panthers. They couldn't score on us, but we couldn't get inside their 10 yard line either.

Midway in the last quarter, Balducci put Knocklemeier in. We worked up a first down on Wilson's 30 with a series of running plays. Then Sousa hit our right end, Dick Petersen, right on the Adams apple with a pass. Petersen, with not a soul near him, dropped it.

The Wilson line guessed right away that Knocklemeier was a passer, and when he faded back on the next play, every Colton receiver was covered. The kid had to eat the ball 20 yards behind scrimmage.

We tried the same play, only this time I nailed the tackle who caught Knocklemeier before. Again all the receivers were covered. I picked myself up and hollered "Run!" The kid took off after me and while the Wilson backs tried to shift gears, Knocklemeier hot-footed it to their 10. I made eight yards on the next play, and Dank smashed into the end zone. Darkner converted, and the game ended that way, Colton, 7; Wilson, 0.

Balducci was plenty happy. Knocklemeier had looked good carrying the ball, we had won—

and the State scouts certainly hadn't found out what a passer the kid was.

The newspapers didn't consider us a wisp of a risk to State's unbeaten team. The only argument was about whether Colton would be able to last through the game.

Each member of the squad felt that the condescension was aimed at him, and each man executed his role as if the Grim Reaper himself were waiting to reward the slackers.

Saturday was made to order for a pass offense, clear and dry with only enough wind to keep the stadium flags from drooping. Balducci started Knocklemeier at quarter. I was to call the plays in the huddle. I figured Coach wanted to run up a score as fast as possible and then protect his lead. There's a psychological advantage in scoring first if you're the underdog. It puts the pressure on the big boys, and when they start trying too hard, they tense up and make mistakes. When we trotted onto the field, I don't think a man in a Colton uniform doubted that we would win.

State won the toss and elected to receive. I chose to defend the south goal, although the choice was meaningless. Darkner's kick was returned to State's 32, and the game was under way. State lost three yards in three running plays, and then punted to Dankowicz on our 25. I saw him tuck the ball under his arm and head north, and I threw a block into a State end bearing down fast. While I was picking myself up, I heard a sudden roar from the crowd. Dank had fumbled. State had recovered.

Here was the break, but it had gone the wrong way. State caught fire. We looked for a running play on their first down, and a pass in the flat caught us looking on vacantly like a delegation of visiting heifers. The State end didn't even get a fingerprint on his trousers as he trotted into the end zone. The conversion was good, and as we moved back to line up for the next kickoff, I saw Balducci's shoulders seemed to have joined his elbows in his raglan sleeves.

We picked up a few yards on running plays, and Knocklemeier clicked on a couple of passes, but we couldn't keep up a sustained attack. We were the ones who were tense and pressing, and things wouldn't go right for us. Only Darkner's inspired punting kept us out of trouble in the first half—that and savage play by our linemen.

Just before the half ended, the State band lined up behind our goalposts, and as we walked toward the locker room, I saw Knocklemeier watch fascinated as the band marched onto the field. It had a whole squad of glockenspiels. Well, four of 'em, anyway.

Balducci didn't have much to say. He just told us to keep doing our best. We felt pretty bad, and just sat there, too big to cry, too sore to laugh. Coach leaned near the door, his chest caved in, looking glum.

Then the door opened, and in skidded Knocklemeier, whacking away at one of the State glockenspiels.

"Get a load of this instrument, Dismal," he said, trotting over to me without noticing the coach. "State has three others just like it. Their director let me try this one."

"Maybe he'll lend the others to the rest of our backfield," Balducci broke in.

Everybody guffawed, except Knocklemeier, who looked a little embarrassed.

"I'll take this back now," he said.

"The heck you will," Balducci snorted. "Hey, Aqua. Take this xylophone out of here. And you, Knocklemeier, hereafter come straight to the dressing room at the half. They don't need you out there in the grounds crew."

Someone hollered in the door that we were due on the field, and we ran out into the sunlight still chuckling over Knocklemeier and the coach.

Darkner ran the kickoff to State's 40. I got 10 yards off tackle, and Dank got another eight on a trap. The State backs still were trying to figure what had happened to their defense against our ground game when Knocklemeier rifled a pass to Ken Eaton, our left end that went for a touchdown. Darkner's kick was wide, but we felt that we were on the way.

As it turned out, our touchdown inspired State, and at the end of the third quarter they led us, 14 to 6. Darkner twisted his knee on the first play of the fourth quarter, and had to be helped from the field. Ed Thorson, who replaced Dark, was fair on defense, but he couldn't punt for sour apples. Knocklemeier read my mind. We couldn't kick out of trouble any more.

"Send 'em deep, Dis," he said, and I decided to give it a try.

On the next play Eaton and I went deep. Knocklemeier's pass dropped into my arms, and we made 25 yards. We tried the same play at the other end, and the State safety man was lucky to break it up. I saw the State's backfield had loosened up, and called for a couple of shovel passes over the line. Knocklemeier couldn't miss.

We scored on a pass to Dankowicz. Thorson attempted the conversion, but missed by five yards. We now trailed by just two points.

But that two point margin might as well have been 50 points when we looked at the clock. There were three minutes left, when we finally had our hands on the ball again.

I called for the deep pass on our first play, and it clicked again, with Eaton carrying the ball out of bounds on State's 45. I started to call

65

for the short passes, just over the line when Knocklemeier interrupted me.

"Dis," he whispered. "I can't pass. That big tackle fell on me and I can barely lift my arm."

If Knocklemeier went out, State wouldn't worry about passes and our ground game would be stopped. If he stayed in, even without passing, we might be able to keep them off balance.

Thorson took the ball on a handoff from Knocklemeier on the next play, and Knocklemeier faked the State line into chasing him to midfield. Thorson went to State's 20 before their safety man nailed him. On three more running plays, we picked up six yards, and, with the clock running out, I dragged out Old Desperation.

OD was a fake field goal attempt. Knocklemeier was in kicking position and I was the holder. The gimmick was for me to keep the ball and either pass or run. It was a play you can't pull more than once a season, and you're lucky if it works once in five seasons. This started out to be one of those noworking times.

Garrott, our center, was weary, maybe. Or maybe he forgot the play. Anyway, when the ball was snapped, it whistled right past my outstretched fingers and into Knocklemeier's hands. With the State line charging in, he couldn't get into position to lateral. He couldn't pass, and a run would be suicide.

Without hesitation, Knocklemeier dropped the

66

ball, and as it touched the ground he kicked it soundly. It soared squarely between the goal posts.

The officials had to confer for several minutes before they announced that the dropkick, though a bit moldy these days, still was a legal scoring weapon and worth three points if successful. When the gun sounded a moment later, the scoreboard read: State, 14; Colton, 15.

Balducci was so happy I thought he was going to cry in the locker room.

"Glockenmeier," he bubbled, "why didn't you tell me that you could dropkick like that?"

"Why, coach," said Knocklemeier, "you never asked me."

"Guess I didn't at that," grinned Balducci. "Well, we'll certainly show 'em next year, with your arm in shape and that toe of yours."

"I meant to tell you about that, too, coach," Knocklemeier said. "I won't be out for football next year."

"What do you mean?" asked Balducci, looking stricken.

"I'm going to transfer to State."

"But you'll lose your eligibility for the season!" Balducci trumpeted.

"Not for the marching band," said Knocklemeier. "They've asked me to play first glockenspiel next fall."

He did, too.

Major Effort

JACK RITCHIE

THE public address system announced that the paid attendance was 53,216 and I wasn't going to argue with that. There didn't seem to be any empty seats at all, not even high up in the stands behind the goal posts.

53,216 people and just about every one of them a stranger.

I mean I come from a small town. Back home, when I was in highschool, I could go onto the football field, look at the stands, and know just about everybody there. Everybody from our town, anyway.

Mom and Dad made a point of being there on the fifty yard line. Especially Dad. He never missed a game. And maybe even my sister, if she got a date who liked to watch football.

Until I came to the university, I never saw

more than three thousand people at one time and that was when Jefferson High played for the regional championship.

I was nervous then, too, but nothing at all like today. Here I was, on the sidelines, walking back and forth to keep warm, and waiting to get out there.

Out on the field, Hesselman barked out the signals and faded back behind the line.

This time there was no blitz and he had time to look for his man. Jennings was out in the open, streaking downfield, two steps behind the man assigned to cover him. Hesselman cocked his arm and threw another long one.

It was a perfect pass, floating down toward Jennings' outstretched arms, but once again it slipped through his fingers. Jennings fell to the ground, pounding the hard turf in frustration.

That made the record only three completions in thirteen attempts and Jennings had muffed five of the passes.

I watched Coach Brewer in front of the bench talking to one of his assistants. Would he take Jennings out?

You really couldn't blame Jennings, I thought. It was just too cold out there today. Only a degree or two above freezing. Not really football weather. Your fingers get stiff and you have trouble holding on to things.

Jennings stayed in.

I tightened my chin strap and double-timed in

69

place for half a minute to keep my legs warm. But mainly I worried about my hands. If a ball hawk like Jennings was having a bad day, it must be rough out there.

The cheer leaders in front of the Ohio stands went into their acrobatic routines to draw some encouragement for their team from the fans. The cheering section flashed its cards—first a diagonal *FIGHT*, and then the cards turned and we got a big O.

Everybody wants to get into the act, I thought.

I felt the tenseness taking hold again, but I knew that I was as ready today as I ever would be.

And I was good. I knew that.

I watched a couple of substitutes throw off their blankets and trot out onto the field.

You don't get good by wishing for it. You aren't born that way. You got to keep working and waiting for your chance. But sometimes you forget that.

I smiled a little as I thought back.

I left highschool figuring that I was something special. When I stepped off the bus at the university, I had the idea that everybody was just marking time and waiting for me to show up.

It didn't take me long to discover that I was just another freshman among a lot of other freshmen who were also big wheels back home.

My eyes went to the players on the field.

Fourth down and three to go. We had the ball

70

on Ohio's seventeen yard line and the score still stood at nothing to nothing.

I looked at Coach Brewer. This was the time to try for the field goal.

But Coach Brewer had his own ideas on how to play the game. He decided to let them try for the first down.

I shook my head and kicked a scrap of paper away from the sidelines.

The quarterback took the ball from center and shoved it into the hands of Schmidt. The big fullback rammed into the line. He picked up a yard, but that wasn't enough. The ball changed sides.

It took a lot of work to be here today. Hard work. A lot more than just showing up on the field on autumn afternoons. The practice went on day after day. Even in summer you couldn't allow yourself to get stale and out of condition.

Back home in the evenings after supper, Dad and I would go out into our big back yard and Dad would coach me.

He was pretty good himself when he went to highschool. If he'd gone on to college he might have become one of the great ones.

On the field, Ohio's right half took the handoff on a sweep. He got one nice block at the line and another as he cut back in at the forty-five.

And then suddenly he was away!

The stands roared as he sped along the sidelines, pursued by the last safety man.

The Ohio back was going to come almost close enough for me to touch—to tackle!

I smiled and quickly stepped back. That would really put my name in the papers, now wouldn't it?

I watched him pull up in the end zone to make the score six to nothing in Ohio's favor.

The teams lined up for the try for the extra point.

The ball was snapped back and held. The kicker swung his leg and the ball went squarely over the crossbar for the extra point.

It looked so smooth and easy from here, I thought. How many people realized how much practice it took to make it look that way?

The teams lined up again for the kick-off and behind them breath vapor steamed from the spectators in the stands.

Yes, I was good, I thought. But even knowing that didn't prevent me from worrying. When I finally got on the field, would I muff a signal? Would my hands become so numb with the cold that I'd mess up something?

My eyes went to the scoreboard clock and my stomach tightened.

Six seconds . . . five . . . four . . . three . . . two . . . one.

The gun officially ended the half.

The teams poured off the field and now I thought the eyes turned to me. All 53,216 pairs of them.

72

I checked the chin strap of my shako again and looked behind me.

They were all waiting, ready with their instruments.

I blew my whistle.

And then strutting high and in full control of my baton, I led the university band onto the football field for the half-time ceremonies.

Everything worked out just fine.

The Quiet Fullback

JACK WOOLGAR

MIKE Conlan leaped high and pulled down a long pass. He tucked the ball under his arm and trotted back to the quarterback.

"Take it easy, pal," Mike said, breathing hard. "This is only the first day of practice and my muscles are still sore from those limbering up exercises the coach gave us. I think I've pinched a nerve."

Jeff Cullen grinned. "In your head, maybe. You're just plain lazy. Give me that ball and get back to work."

"No way. At least not until you answer a couple of questions. First, how're our chances for another title this year, and second, who's our fullback replacement?"

"If I could answer your second question I might be able to answer your first. Our reserves

74

aren't much good. Even Coach Maxwell hasn't made up his mind."

"Probably can't find anyone to suit your exclusive bunch."

Jeff frowned. "Quit calling us exclusive. We accepted you, didn't we?"

"Since I'm six five, weigh one ninety-seven, and run the hundred in nine six, you didn't have a choice," Mike said dryly. "My sticky fingers made you look good. But suppose coach picks a coal miner's son? Does he get the silent treatment?"

"Why not?" Jeff said coolly. "Your credentials were acceptable. But a coal miner! You've got to be kidding."

Mike shook his head. "I've played with your gang for a year and I still don't understand your attitudes. Why this exclusive stuff?"

"We've been raised in an exclusive neighborhood. In fact, the only reason we attend Mumford is because our fathers did. Thank goodness this is my last year in this second rate college."

Ordinarily, Mike would have made a snappy retort. Instead, he pointed downfield to where a tall, broad shouldered youth was kicking field goals.

"Did you see that?" Mike sputtered. "Watch that big guy at the kicking tee. He just booted a forty-five yarder."

"So what? Anyone can get lucky. Go ahead and watch him. I'll get Pete to take your place."

Mike handed over the football. "Fine. If you're not curious, I am. Hope he doesn't turn out to be another rich man's son." With this parting shot, Mike walked downfield.

He watched the husky kicker split the uprights again and then said, "Nice going, kid. Newcomer, aren't you? I'm Mike Conlan, first string wide receiver."

They shook hands and the stranger said in a soft, mild voice, "My name is Olaf Knudson. Transfer from Merlin College."

With an admiring glance at Olaf's muscular body, Mike said, "I can see you've played football before. What position?"

"Field goal specialist and fullback."

"That figures. By the way, what's your father's occupation?"

"He's a miner," was the proud answer. "Why do you ask?"

Mike chuckled. "You'll soon find out. Wait until you meet our exclusive gang."

"Exclusive! I don't understand."

"You will. They are all seniors on our first team offensive unit. Used to be seven of them until last year's fullback cracked up his expensive roadster and landed in the hospital. Trouble is, they are really fine athletes and top football players even though they act like snobs."

Olaf looked puzzled. "Why are they snobs?"

"Money! You are out of their class since your

father is only a coal miner. Just ignore them. Took them some time to accept me."

Mike thought he saw a faint twinkle in Olaf's blue eyes. But the fullback only said mildly, "Since I'm out of their class I'll have to try harder. And I still have to convince your coach that I'm a good fullback."

"I'm convinced without even seeing you play. How much do you weigh?"

"About two twenty-five."

Mike grinned. "That ought to get you places in a hurry. Let's go over and meet Jeff and his gang. He's the ringleader. If he accepts you, the others will too. But don't count on it."

Jeff and his five cronies were tossing a pigskin back and forth when Mike and Olaf approached them. "Hey, Jeff!" Mike said in his usual brash manner. "Stop pretending you're a football player. I want you to meet your new fullback, Olaf Knudson."

Ignoring Olaf completely, Jeff said, "Who says so, you or Coach Maxwell?"

Mike shrugged. "I say so, and I'm a pretty good judge. I sort of figured your eyes were getting weaker when you threw that pass over my head. You can't recognize a good fullback when you see one."

"You talk too much, Mike." Then, looking at Olaf for the first time, Jeff said abruptly, "How come you enrolled at Mumford?"

"They have a good engineering course," was the quiet answer.

"Engineering, huh? That your father's line of work?"

"No. He's a miner."

"So you're a coal miner's son," Jeff said with a condescending air. "That's strange. With your name your ancestors must have been Vikings. So we'll call you Vike, providing you make the team."

Jeff turned his back on the newcomer without bothering to introduce his teammates. Olaf's face was expressionless.

"Come on, Olaf," Mike growled. "The only way to show up these six snobs is to play super football. In the meantime you'll get to meet some sociable guys. Their fathers work for a living."

Olaf just smiled. But as they left the field, Mike said, "Why didn't you tell Jeff off? A big guy like you should be more aggressive. Don't tell me you're afraid of that bunch of snobs."

"I've never been afraid of anyone," was the quiet answer. "As for being aggressive, I can be that too, once I get my hands on a football."

Mike slapped Olaf's shoulder. "That's the old spirit. After you go into action, those misfits will have to accept you. After all, they want another title. And since they are seniors, this is their last chance."

But to Mike's disgust, the six snobs didn't

78

The Quiet Fullback

change their attitude even after Olaf proved his ability in scrimmage. The powerful fullback was so far superior to the other candidates that there was no comparison. He tore big holes through the line even though openings were small or non-existent.

"What's the matter with you guys?" Mike demanded hotly after one lackluster scrimmage. "How come the tackles and guards don't wipe out the defense? Does Olaf always have to make his own holes?"

"You don't like my quarterbacking," Jeff sniffed, "talk to the coach. He's running the team, not you."

"Oh, sure," Mike retorted. "What good would that do? Coach probably figures you guys are over-confident; that you'll get going once the season opens. Well, I'll tell you something, Jeff. If you guys don't wake up, you can forget about another title. Most of our opposition is weak, with the exception of Clarkville. They have the best pass defense in the league and without a good ground game we're sunk."

Jeff had no answer to Mike's tirade. The quarterback merely shrugged as the coach sent in his second team.

Just as Mike predicted, matters became worse after the season opened. Teamwork was spotty and some games were won by a scant margin. Olaf, in his quiet manner, tried hard to break the aloof barrier. But in spite of his bull-like

79

rushes and uncomplaining manner, he was still ostracized by the class-conscious six.

Halfway through the season, they tangled with Clarkville, a young, determined team. They had won all their games with a tricky offense and a strong defensive unit. Their loyal rooters loudly proclaimed that their team would stop Mumford's drive to another title.

Clarkville won the toss and elected to receive. A speedy runner caught the ball on the five and ran it back to the forty. Five plays later Clarkville scored. Their rooters went wild.

When Mumford got the ball, a pass to Mike and an end sweep by a wingback, brought the ball to the midstripe. Then Jeff fumbled and an alert Clarkville back recovered. A pass on first down rang up another score. The kick was good and it was a 14-0 game at the end of the first quarter.

The two teams battled on even terms in the second quarter. Then, with two minutes showing on the clock, Mumford brought the ball down to the Clarkville thirty yard line. Two passes were knocked down and an off tackle slant was smothered.

In the huddle Jeff snapped, "Okay, Vike. Let's see if your educated toe can get us on the board."

Although the kick was at an angle, Olaf made it good. Mike said, "That's booting 'em, pal." Jeff and his pals made no comment.

With forty seconds showing on the clock,

Mumford kicked off. The usually sure-fingered Clarkville receiver misjudged the ball and fumbled it on the fifteen yard line. An alert Mumford player scooped it up and was nailed on the twelve. Twenty-five seconds left.

In the huddle, Jeff looked at Olaf. "No way we can make up that yardage in a few seconds. Okay, hotshot, let's see you give us another three points."

Olaf said quietly. "I can do a hundred in nine six. Fake a field goal and give me the ball. I'll get it over."

He did! With Clarkville set for the three pointer, Olaf exploded through the surprised opposition. He spun and battered his way over the goal line with two defenders trying to drag him down. The whistle ended the half a second later.

The Mumford stands came alive, but Mike paid no attention to the noise. His eyes were on Olaf, who was still sprawled motionless on the ground. Mike was bending over the big fullback when Coach Maxwell and the trainer rushed up.

The trainer's probing fingers brought a groan from Olaf. He opened his eyes and struggled to a sitting position. "I'm okay," he said softly. "Just had the wind knocked out of me."

Coach Maxwell said, "We'll find out when you get on the rubbing table." Turning to the trainer, the coach snapped, "Have Doc look him over and report to me."

Then, supported by the coach and trainer, Olaf

walked off the field. Mike waited until a sub kicked the extra point and then hurried to the locker room. Olaf was sitting up on the rubbing table while the trainer was taping the fullback's ribs.

"What did Doc say?" Mike demanded. "Couple of cracked ribs?"

Olaf shook his head. "Just a few bruises," he whispered.

"Then why all the tapes?"

Both the trainer and Olaf smiled. "You'll find out in the next half," he whispered. "Sometimes you have to use a little strategy to make a team fight. Just let them think my ribs are cracked."

Jeff got up from one of the benches and walked over to the rubbing table. He stared glumly at the tape around Olaf's body. "Sorry you got banged up, Vike," he said grudgingly. "And thanks for the touchdown. We're only four points behind, but it might as well be twenty. I was counting on you for a couple of field goals. But with you out of there . . . well, your replacement doesn't have the punch."

Olaf remained silent after Jeff's partial apology. Mike didn't. "So you finally realize that Olaf is a star fullback. Too bad you didn't wake up before." With a sly wink at Olaf, Mike said, "Take it easy, kid. If we're lucky, maybe I can hang onto one of Jeff's passes. Or maybe Clarkville will get over-confident and oblige us with a couple of fumbles."

Mike joined his teammates in the other room just as the door opened and Coach Maxwell entered. Instead of the usual pep talk, he went to the blackboard and wrote, Clarkville 14, Mumford 10. Gloomy silence settled over the team as the coach closed the door behind him.

When the team trotted onto the field to start the third quarter, Olaf got a big hand as he limped to the players' bench.

The third quarter started out much like the first. Clarkville scored the first time they got their hands on the football. A few minutes later they got close enough for an easy field goal. Now it was a 24-10 game, with the once mighty Mumford team on the short end of the score.

Then a long pass to Mike brought the ball into Clarkville territory. But Mumford's running backs got nowhere and the pigskin changed hands.

Back on the bench, Mike whispered to the blanketed Olaf, "I don't know what kind of strategy you cooked up, but you'd better start using it. We only have a little over a quarter to score fourteen points for a tie, and seventeen for a win. Sometimes I wish you'd talk more instead of being so quiet."

"Patience, Mike," Olaf said softly. "Things will start popping when we change goals."

It was still 24-10 when the quarter ended with the ball in possession of Mumford on their thirty yard stripe. Mike was moving back into the huddle when he saw Olaf running out. The big full-back wasn't limping.

"Give me the ball on the first play," Olaf said firmly to the open-mouthed Jeff. "And keep on alternating between me and Mike. Coach's orders."

"You can't be serious, Olaf!" Jeff protested. "You could injure yourself permanently." The rest of the superior six added their voices to the protest.

"Come on, let's go!" Mike warned. "Unless you want a five yard penalty for stalling."

The two teams lined up and when the ball was snapped, Mike faked a short pass and cut over in time to see Olaf burst through a big hole between tackle and guard. The big fullback thundered all the way to the Clarkville forty before he was hauled down.

Back in the huddle, Olaf said quietly, "Give me the ball again, Jeff. Same play only on the other side of the line. You can try a pass next."

Mike could hardly believe his ears when Jeff said mildly, "Okay, Olaf. And you guys," he added, pointing to the other pair of guard and tackle, "had better open up a hole. Don't let Clarkville lay a hand on Olaf."

"So that's the strategy," Mike muttered under his breath. "Protect a badly injured but game team member. Sure has made a change in Jeff; he even forgot to use the word Vike."

The lines crouched. Again Olaf got the ball.

84

Legs churning, he broke into the open and made another first down. Then on the next play, with Clarkville drawn up close, Mike snatched a pass from between two defenders, and raced across the goal for a touchdown. Mumford rooters roared their approval.

The touchdown put new zip into Mumford's defense and after the kickoff, they held Clarkville for no gain, forcing them to kick.

A Mumford return specialist was downed on the twenty-five and Olaf went to work again. Sheer power got him twelve yards. Another slant through tackle and Olaf carried to midstripe. With the Mumford rooters screaming for another touchdown, Jeff mixed up short passes and Olaf's plunges to get the team down to the twenty yard line.

In the huddle, Olaf said, "I'm not the only ball carrier on this team. Give one of our backs a chance."

"Sorry, Olaf. I guess I have been working you and Mike too hard. But we need this game and I'm going with the winning combination."

But the ball went to a back and, perhaps inspired by Olaf's heroics, the senior back got down to the two. The same back went through a hole opened up by Olaf, and scored. The kick was good and the score was tied, 24-24.

Sitting on the bench, Mike mopped his forehead and looked at the quiet fullback. "How about it, Olaf. Can we get the go ahead touch-down?"

Olaf shrugged. "I think so. But can our defense hold? If the Clarkville quarterback elects to eat up the clock with a ground game until they get within kicking range we might not have enough time for another touchdown."

It was a shrewd guess. The aroused Clarkville team returned the kickoff to their thirty-five, and then went to work. Alternating with rushes and side-line passes, they got inside Mumford terri-tory. A roughing penalty cost Clarkville fifteen, but a long pass on first down erased the penalty and gave them first down on Mumford's thirty-five. And the minutes were ticking away!

In spite of a stubborn Mumford defense, Clarkville ground out another first down and the ball was on the twenty-five. Another touch-down would leave Mumford struggling to eke out a tie.

Somehow, the Mumford defense rose to the occasion. They turned back two line smashes and batted down a pass. Clarkville had to go for the field goal.

The angle wasn't too difficult, and Mike watched the ball sail over the uprights. Clark-ville rooters jumped up and down. Mike looked at the clock and shook his head. Only a minute and a half left! Perhaps time enough for a tieing field goal, but a winning touchdown? He jammed on his helmet and grumbled to Olaf, "Now's your chance to be a hero, pal. If you can break through their defense and score, the school will erect a statue in your honor."

"Don't overlook Jeff's accurate passes. They cover a lot of ground in a hurry."

Jeff, with an eye on the clock, had the same idea. After the kickoff was brought back to the thirty, a pass to the tall wide receiver gained sixteen yards. A pass to the tight end was almost intercepted. Then Olaf battled his way to the Clarkville thirty-five where a swarm of defenders pulled him down. He got up, clutching his side. Less than a minute left.

"Still faking cracked ribs?" Mike said on the way back to the huddle. "You don't have to, pal. The exclusive bunch is on your side now. Just break away for a TD and watch those six guys really crack your ribs."

Olaf didn't waste his breath in a reply.

"Another first down and a pass should do it," Jeff said in the huddle. "Get us another down, Olaf, and I'll call a pass to Mike without a huddle. I think we can make it."

Mike glanced at the clock. Twenty-five seconds left! Olaf might go all the way, but if he didn't! Would there be time enough left for a pass?

The ball was snapped and Mike headed for the corner, hoping to fool the defense. He glanced back over his shoulder; just in time to see the pigskin sailing toward him. Mike leaped, twisted,

87

and spun over the goal line. The kick was perfect and Mumford had the lead, 31-24. The clock showed ten seconds left!

That was the game, because Clarkville's desperation passes were batted down. Jubilant Mumford fans poured onto the field and Mike and Olaf were carried off the field by happy teammates.

In the locker room Mike said, "What inspired you to throw a pass I wasn't expecting? How did you know I would turn around in time to catch it? You took an awful chance, pal."

"Time," Olaf replied quietly. "And a cracked rib. I was tackled pretty hard on my last carry."

Just then the door burst open and a heavy-set, well-dressed man strode over to Olaf. "Heard you were injured, son, in the first half. Why did the coach let you back in the game? What happened?"

"Wasn't hurt in the first half, Dad. Got roughed up a few minutes ago; think a rib is cracked. Nothing to worry about."

Ignoring the stranger, Jeff said, "You mean to say you didn't get your ribs cracked in the first half. Then why were you taped up?"

Olaf managed a weak grin. "Thought it might give me some protection; at least more than I had been getting."

Jeff and his teammates exchanged sheepish grins.

"And now," Olaf said proudly, "I'd like you

to meet my Dad. He owns the biggest copper mine in Arizona."

"Copper mine!" Jeff sputtered. "I thought you said you were the son of a coal miner."

This time Olaf's grin widened. "I never said anything about a coal mine. You just jumped to conclusions. But you are partly right. Dad was a coal miner in his younger days."

Olaf's father laughed. "I don't know what this is all about, but I'll get it out of my son. Now have the Doc look at your rib, Olaf. Then later I'll treat the bunch to a steak dinner."

Jeff shook hands with Mr. Knudson and said earnestly, "We acted like a bunch of snobs, but we're cured. And with Clarkville out of the way, we're a cinch to win another title . . . if Olaf doesn't get too tricky."

Mr. Knudson laughed again. "Don't ever trust a quiet fullback. They do the most damage."

The Almost Magic Toe

◆ ◆ ◆ ◆ ◆

JACK RITCHIE

I THOUGHT the new men looked just about average. Only one was much taller than anybody else—even us seniors. And he looked about 30 pounds heavier than any of the rest of the squad.

Coach Nelson's eyes lit up. "What's your name?"

"James Hackett, sir."

"I haven't seen you around, Hackett. Freshman?"

"No, sir. I'm a senior. I transferred from Iron River High. It's up north, sir. Near the state line."

The coach nodded. "What position did you play?"

"We didn't have a football team, sir. Iron River is the smallest high school in the state. Not big enough to have a football team."

I didn't think the coach would put him in the line. We've got the finest line in the state—defensively, at least—and there's no sense in tampering with the best.

But with Hackett's size, I felt sure he'd be right for fullback. And the team could use one.

Milton Elderidge, the sports editor of the school paper, says the team really needs a fullback—and a right half—and a left half—and quarterback.

I'm the quarterback.

We don't have such a bad team. Last season only 28 points were scored against us.

But our record for the seven games was no wins, two ties, and five losses.

And we didn't score a touchdown. Not even a field goal. We lost two games by the score of 7 to 0, two games 6 to 0, and one 2 to 0. The tie games ended 0 to 0.

We moved the ball pretty well in spots. We averaged 162 yards rushing per game and I completed 64 percent of my passes to lead the league.

Everything clicked, *until* we got well into our opponent's territory. Then everything went wrong.

Milt Elderidge says we're a team with a lot of color. All of it gray.

The next afternoon, the coach said, "Hackett, we'll try you at fullback."

I called the first team into a huddle. "Hackett,

91

we'll try 3-A-3 first. A plain handoff and you drive between right tackle and right guard."

He nodded. "I got it."

Our team works from the T, and I took the ball direct from under the center, heeled back, turned, and slipped the ball to Hackett as he came by.

Our right guard and right tackle wedged open a nice lane.

But by the time Hackett got there, a lot of people were waiting to meet him. He lost about a yard.

Back in the huddle, I said, "Hackett, you've got to hustle more."

He looked offended. "I *did*."

"We'll try 3-B-3," I said. "Same as the last one, only through the left side."

This time I shoveled the ball to Hackett and stepped clear.

It took five men to bring him down, but he still lost two yards.

Coach Nelson walked out onto the field. "Hackett, why didn't you tell me you were so slow?"

Hackett shifted uneasily. "I didn't *know* I was slow. I never played football before, so I never had anybody to compare myself with."

Poor Hackett, so big and strong, and yet all that manpower was wasted because he couldn't put one foot in front of the other.

"But I can kick, sir," Hackett said.

Coach sighed. "All right. Let's see you kick."

"Where to?"

The coach laughed. "Try to hit one of those goal posts."

They were about fifty yards downwind.

"Which one?" Hackett asked.

Coach looked at him a little sharply. "Hit the right-side one. Make it four feet ten and three-quarter inches above the ground."

Hackett squinted down the field, took his step, and his foot connected.

The ball hit the right-hand goal post about seven feet off the ground.

Hackett frowned. "I underestimated the wind at my back, sir."

Coach didn't say a word, just nodded to Hackett to try another.

Hackett kicked six more times—and hit the goal post six times. Then Coach made me trot up and down the sidelines, laying down a handkerchief for Hackett to aim at.

Out of twenty kicks, Hackett missed the handkerchief only twice—those times the distance was over sixty yards—and even then he didn't miss by more than a foot.

We quit practice when it got too dark to see anything but the smile on the coach's face.

It didn't take much imagination to figure out how much Hackett was going to mean to the team.

We had the best defensive team in the conference last year, allowing an average of only four points per game. And this year we had practically the same line from end to end.

Maybe we couldn't push the ball over the goal line, but this year we wouldn't *have* to. All we needed was to get the ball near our opponent's 40-yard line. From that distance we could count on Hackett to get us three points with a field goal. We ought to get that close seven or eight times in a game.

As practice continued, Milton Elderidge began coming to watch the team and get information for his column. He walked over to me one day while I was taking a breather on the bench.

"I suppose you expect to win all your games with field goals?" he said in a sarcastic tone of voice.

"What's wrong with that?"

"I thought you had more pride."

"What's pride got to do with it?"

He shrugged. "If I were on an offensive team that had no offense, it would bother me."

"Well, don't let it keep you awake nights. You're not on the team."

Hackett asked about the canvas-covered mound near the 50-yard line.

"That's our cannon. We fire a blank every time the team scores a touchdown," Elderidge said. "It hasn't been fired in more than a year. The barrel's probably rusty."

I glared at him. "It is not."

94

"Well, it won't have a chance to get rusty this season," Hackett said.

Eldridge still looked gloomy. "The cannon isn't fired for field goals. Only touchdowns. It's a school tradition."

That Saturday afternoon we met Jefferson High.

Prentiss, our left half, took the opening kick-off on the nine and brought it back to the 30 before he was downed.

On the first play from scrimmage, I faded back and tossed one to the left end. He pulled it in on the Jefferson 48 and got nailed in his tracks. But it was a first down.

On third and two, I fired a short pass to Wittich, but he let it slip away.

It was fourth and two on the Jefferson 40; Hackett trotted onto the field.

As we shifted into field goal formation, I don't think there was a man on the Jefferson team who wasn't positive that we were going to fake.

When Hackett swung his leg, the ball rose and sailed right between the uprights.

Our line held Jefferson—and after a long drive we stalled on their 24.

The field goal was easy for Hackett—another three-pointer. At game's end, the score was 24 to 0. Hackett had kicked eight field goals to set a conference record.

Of course, most of us were delighted at winning our first game in more than a year. But not

Elderidge. He looked gloomy. I tried to shrug off the uneasy feeling that our victory might have been a freak, an accident. But I couldn't.

When the school paper came out on Wednesday, Elderidge had praise for Hackett and for our defensive unit, but his last line really hurt. "The offensive platoon appeared on the field at regular intervals—mostly to keep the Jefferson players from feeling lonely."

That Saturday, we took Monitor, 21 to 0. The week after, Roosevelt went down, 18 to 6. Next, we clobbered Delaven Tech, 27 to 0. Hackett's toe accounted for all of our points.

At practice before the next game, I noticed Hackett walk over to the cannon at the 50-yard line. He took the canvas off one end and looked down the barrel.

I joined him.

"Rust," he said.

"Not much." I put my arm in the barrel and rubbed at the spot with my sleeve.

Hackett looked thoughtful. "Have you *ever* heard it fired?"

My face got red. "Sure. When I was a sophomore on the third team."

That Saturday we took on Rutherford High, and with less than one minute left, we were ahead 18 to 7. It was third down, with eight yards to go, on our opponent's 13.

Wittich took my pass just in bounds on the

96

sidelines about two yards beyond the line of scrimmage.

It looked as if he could scamper for the first down, maybe even drive for a TD.

But he whirled and recrossed the scrimmage line. He ran behind it to a point about midway between the sidelines and then tried to drive straight ahead like a fullback.

He lost two yards.

Fourth and ten, and Hackett ran onto the field.

He glared at Wittich. "Why didn't you go for the first down? You might've even gone all the way after you caught the pass."

Wittich shifted a little. "But suppose I *didn't* make the first down? We'd have had the ball right near the sidelines on fourth down. You would have had an almost impossible kicking angle."

"So you sacrificed a first down—maybe a touchdown—just so that I would have a better kicking position?"

"Why not? A *positive* three points is better than a *maybe* six."

We went into formation. Hackett booted. The ball slewed off to the left. Hackett blinked and his mouth dropped.

The game ended, 18 to 7.

When we trotted off the field, I looked toward the press table. Elderidge was glaring. Mostly at Wittich.

During practice the next week, I noticed that

97

a lot of Hackett's kicks were going to the left or the right of the goal posts.

I began to get a cold feeling. Was he getting stale, or falling into a slump?

On Saturday we met the Merris Falls Trojans.

They won the toss and elected to receive. Hackett boomed the kickoff over the end zone—as usual—and the Trojans took over on their own 20.

We had figured them for the T, but they came out single wing, and moved the ball fairly well, getting three first downs in a row.

And then, on second down and six on our 27, our defensive team suddenly found itself looking at the I formation. Before it could adjust, the Trojan quarterback fired a long looper into the corner of the end zone where a Merris Falls end waited to haul it in.

The point after was missed, but the score was 6 to 0.

During the first half, we never managed to get the ball downfield far enough for field goal position, but Hackett had the chance to boom some nice long punts.

When we trotted onto the field for the second half, we weren't particularly worried. The Trojan defense was playing way over its head and that couldn't last. The records showed that.

Besides, it seemed like a cinch for us to move the ball into field goal territory at least half a dozen times in the next two quarters.

98

Olson, our right half, took the kick-off all the way down to the Merris Falls 19 before he was caught.

The next two plays netted five. On third and five I faded back.

The line held and I had time to see Wittich all alone in the end zone.

I cocked my arm.

And then a lot of things flashed through my mind.

Suppose Wittich dropped the ball? If he *did* drop it, we'd have fourth down with the ball in an awkward position for Hackett's field goal try.

Wittich's words came back to me. "A *positive* three points is better than a *maybe* six."

I tucked the ball under my arm and angled toward my left. I was caught, and lost four yards, but that didn't matter. We had the ball squarely in front of the goal posts.

When Hackett came into the huddle, he spoke to me. "Wittich was in the clear. Didn't you see him?"

I explained my strategy and expected him to nod approvingly. He didn't.

I propped the ball and Hackett stepped into it. The kick was no good, and Hackett was silent as he walked off the field.

When we finally got the ball back, we picked up a first down. On the next sequence of plays I kept the calls through the center of the line or off tackle.

We went no place and had fourth and six on the Merris 33. But the ball lay in front of the goal posts again and that was what I'd been aiming for.

Hackett came in. "Conway, their defense was pulled in on each of those last three plays. They were expecting you to try the line. Why didn't you sweep wide or go for a pass?"

I felt my ears redden. *"I'm* the quarterback on this team; *I* call the plays."

This time Hackett's try for the field goal went way off to the left.

The clock ticked on until there were only six minutes to play. We got another fourth down on the Merris 26. Right in front of the goal posts. . . .

Hackett *had* to make this one! And if we could get possession of the ball once more, we might at least tie.

When Hackett came in, he called for a time out.

He looked us over. "This time we're going to fake the kick."

"Fake?" I asked.

He nodded. "That's what Coach wants."

I frowned. "Is there something wrong with your foot?"

"No," he said evenly. "But there's *plenty* wrong with this team. Last year you didn't score a single touchdown. That's unusual, but it's possible. The point is that last year you were *trying.*"

His eyes skipped from face to face. "This year,

100

you haven't even tried. Your only aim is to get the ball in a position so that I can kick a field goal. This team is a one-man team. *Me.*"

A sudden suspicion crossed my mind. "Did you deliberately miss those kicks?"

"No. I have my bad days, too." Then he glared at us. "Are you *afraid* to score a touchdown?"

"All right," I snapped. "Let's get on with the play."

The ball came back to where I crouched on one knee. I went back and to my right with the ball. Hackett moved in front of me for any blocking that might have to be done.

The play caught the Merris team off guard. I had the choice of two open receivers in the end zone, and Wittich took the pass with ease.

Central High had scored its first touchdown in two years.

The crowd exploded into the loudest roar I've ever heard. Suddenly I realized something.

I hadn't heard the cannon fired.

I called time out and trotted over to where Milton Elderidge stood beside the gun. Another one of his jobs was to fire it.

"How come I didn't hear anything?" I asked.

He flushed. "I forgot to bring out the blanks. They're in the locker room." He got even redder. "I never thought we'd need them."

I almost choked. I couldn't say a word. I just pointed.

I guess my look scared Elderidge, because he

101

ran off the field toward the locker room as if he were competing in the 100-yard dash.

The referee came over to see what was holding up our try for the extra point. When I told him, he called an official time out.

We waited. Everybody on the field, and in the stands, waited.

When Elderidge came rushing back onto the field, he toted half a dozen blanks. Just to be on the safe side, I guess.

And when that cannon finally boomed, I *knew* it wasn't the last time we'd hear it. It made such a nice noise.

Monday Morning
Quarterback

M. G. OGAN

I WAS sitting in my office under the concrete grandstand we call Dixon High School Stadium with my head in my hands that Monday morning in late November. My football team had just lost their 8th game Friday night and coming up was Homecoming. Next Friday night we faced the league champions, Newhall High's blue-shirted Tigers. Joe Nethery coaches Newhall. I was second-string quarterback behind Joe for three years at Louisiana State University.

I'm Johnny Muller, Dixon's head coach, and Bill Fitzsimmons from Purdue is my assistant. Both of us were assistant coaches until Buck Walters suddenly retired in mid-season, complaining about his ulcers.

I'd lost my first and second string quarterbacks trying to beat Willow Springs High Friday night.

103

My first string quarterback had broken his wrist. My second stringer was sacked the second time he called a play and dislocated his shoulder. That ran me out of quarterbacks. I sent in plays the rest of the game. We still lost 14-21. So Willow Springs players went home happy. They'd won their first game of the season.

Which will give you an idea about the kind of Dixon team Fitz and I were coaching. But I don't believe in throwing off on my players. They were a bunch of hard-trying sophomores and juniors. We didn't have a senior on the squad.

I was trying to decide who we should switch over to quarterback when Fitz came in. He's a round-faced 230-pounder usually beaming optimism regardless of circumstances but this morning he wore a puzzled frown.

"Do you know that sophomore kid who just transferred here from Ruston High?" Fitz asked. "Jerry Huff is his name."

"Sure. He's in one of my Social Studies classes. Big kid, dark brown hair, clumsy as the devil, but a straight A student?"

Fitz nodded. "That's the boy. He wants to play quarterback against the Newhall Tigers. Jerry says we can win the game and while he was telling me this I almost believed him."

"Jerry must talk a good football game."

"You can make up your own mind about that," Fitz said, "because I told him to come over here and talk with you."

Fitz left because he had a Chemistry class. Jerry Huff knocked and came into my office.

"Sit down," I said. "Tell me about it."

"When I found out I was coming over here, Coach, I watched every game Dixon has played. I also know something about the Newhall Tigers. A cousin of mine plays for them. If you'll let me quarterback this Friday night we can beat them."

Newhall's season record was: 42-0, 54-6, 37-3, 45-0, 31-7, 63-0, 27-14, and 51-6. Yet ours is a tough league that fields some of the best football teams in the state.

Dixon's record stood at: 0-23, 5-20, 6-28, 0-34, 14-20, 7-28, 14-20, 14-21.

I stared at Jerry running those figures through my mind. "What make you think you can play football?"

"I've studied the game and practiced."

"Let's go out on the field and see if you can throw a pass."

"Sure. Let's do that."

When we were on the field and I'd handed him the ball I said, "I'm going to run a down and out pattern. Make it a bomb."

"Sure, Coach, whatever you say."

I left Jerry on the ten and sprinted to the fifty yard line before I turned and looked for the ball. If I'd had numbers on my chest he would have hit them. It was a rifle-shot pass and nearly knocked the wind out of me.

"Let's try that again," I said when I'd trotted

back down the field and handed Jerry the ball. "I'll go deeper this time."

"Sure, Coach. I'll throw left-handed this time."

I sprinted sixty yards before I made my move. The ball was delivered right into my outstretched hands.

I tucked the ball under my arm and walked back to Jerry. "Question, Jerry," I said. "Where did you learn to throw a football like that?"

"In summer camp."

"You'd better let me have the name of that camp. I may want to go there myself."

"Dad will get you in for their coaches clinic."

"And just who is your father?"

"You may have heard of him. Lloyd Huff who used to play for Oklahoma. He's one of the assistant backfield coaches for the Green Bay Packers now."

Lloyd Huff was a three-time All American at the University of Oklahoma when Bud Wilkinson was coaching there.

"I've been going to the Packer summer camp with Dad since I was seven."

I put my hand on his shoulder. "Suit-up and come out for practice tonight," I said. "Does anyone else know who your father is?"

"No, sir."

"Let's keep it that way."

"Do you think I have a chance of playing Friday night?"

106

"It's a possibility," I told him. I gave Jerry my play book. "Look it over in study hall."

I told Fitz about Jerry at lunch. "If he can call plays and run like he throws a football," I said, "we've got us a secret weapon against Newhall. He could have made the difference earlier this season."

It's hard to explain what practice was like that Monday afternoon. The team was suited up in sweatshirts and sweatpants for a light drill.

I had to introduce Jerry because most of the team didn't know him yet. "Now let's run some plays but no hard blocking," I said. "We'll scrimmage Tuesday and Wednesday."

A team is usually down and lethargic after losing a game. But the minute Jerry lined up behind the center and barked signals something happened.

In my office after practice Fitz tried to explain it. "It's as if you've been sweating out a music school recital and then a master pianist sits down to play."

Before calling his plays Jerry would say, "We're going to beat the Tigers."

The linemen were off the ball on cue. My backs ran their hearts out. It was only brush blocking but no one missed their man.

Passing was a problem. Jerry delivered the

107

ball too hot for our receivers to handle. I had a word with him about that in the locker room.

"Can you throw a softer pass, Jerry?" I asked. "You're on target every time but these kids don't have the hands to handle your stuff."

"If I start lobbing the ball I'll be intercepted. Newhall's defensive backs have been grabbing off forward passes all season. I don't want that to happen Friday night."

"Let's work with your receivers tomorrow," I said. "Keep throwing as you have."

"Coach?"

"Yes?"

"Newhall has been defensing the Single Wing Back and Double Wing Back formations all season. They've never seen the Wing T."

"You're suggesting we switch over this late in the season?"

"Just an idea," Jerry said. "A few basic plays off the Wing T could do the job."

I talked it over with Fitz. "The kid is husky enough to be the spinning fullback we'd need to make the Wing T go," I told him. You need a quarterback who can run, throw, and fake to make the Wing T work.

The quarterback plays directly behind the center and handles the ball every play. The fullback is behind him with the left halfback three long steps to his left. The right halfback plays just outside his own end and close to the line of scrimmage.

108

When he has the ball the quarterback can fake handoffs to all three of his other backs; then run with the ball or drop back and pass. Or he can give the ball to his fullback or halfbacks.

It's a nightmare to defense. It's also a hard offense to learn. The key is your quarterback.

Fitz is usually conservative but he said, "Let's use it. Jerry's good enough to make it go and the kids are with him."

Tuesday, Wednesday, and Thursday practice sessions were devoted to the Wing T. I counted on getting some complaints from the team, expecting them to learn a new offensive formation coming up to their final game of the season, but they were bubbling with enthusiasm.

"Come on, let's get it right, we're going to win," Jerry kept telling them. "Let's *go*, Tiger Eaters!"

My pep talk Friday evening was short. "These so-called Tigers may be overconfident tonight," I told the team, "but don't think they can't bite you. Just go out there confident you can win. Each one of you is outweighed by at least ten pounds. The Tigers are coming off a long winning streak. But Fitz and I are betting you can do the job."

While the rest of the team trotted out on the field Jerry stayed back for a word with me. "Are you going to send in plays or am I in charge, Coach?"

I looked at him. He was excited but not too tense. I somehow knew this kid wasn't going to

109

lose his poise. "If I do send in a play," I told him, "you can use it or not. You'll be closer to the action than I am."

"Thanks, Coach." He patted my shoulder and went out on the field after the team.

I joined Fitz on the bench. We watched the Tigers warming up. They were big and looked mean. Could our crimson-shirted kids handle these blue-shirted champions? There was a sinking sensation in my stomach.

"I suddenly don't feel so good," I told Fitz.

Joe Nethery is cocky. While we waited for the toss he came over to shake hands. "We'll try not to run up too big a score on you, Johnny."

"That's thoughtful, Joe," I said. "Real thoughtful."

"I'm starting my second team," he said.

"Well, thank you. Nice to give your first string a rest."

"Sure." Joe grinned and patted my shoulder. "See you after the game."

I'd named Jerry acting captain for this game. We won the toss and he elected to receive.

Now all my other backs were instructed to stay away from any kickoff that would roll into the end zone. But I hadn't mentioned this to Jerry. He was deep man on our ten. It was a booming kickoff, bound for the end zone, but Jerry made a leaping catch.

It caught the Tiger wedge by surprise. Jerry went right through them, swiveling out of tackles, and was in the clear. It was their kicker who blocked him out of bounds on their forty-five yard line.

Jerry brought the team up to the line without a huddle. I saw Joe Nethery stand up when he spotted that Wing T. His defensive backs were thrown off stride by it.

The ball was snapped, Jerry faked to the fullback; then dropped back. Tight end Lou Weitzel was in the clear downfield. He had the confused Tiger cornerback by at least three strides.

Ducking away from a charging lineman Jerry threw to him left-handed.

Lou juggled the ball while my heart missed a few beats; got control and raced into the end zone.

Jerry waved off the place-kicker I started to send in. Another pass to Weitzel who'd scampered to the corner of the end zone with no one near him and we were leading 8-0.

Joe Nethery sent his first team in to receive our kickoff. Fitz groaned. "Now the slaughter begins."

"Kicking to them may be our first mistake this game," I said.

Jerry said something to our kicker while we were lining up. It was a squib kick awkwardly fielded by a husky tackle. Jerry slammed into him with a head-on flying tackle, popping the ball out of his arms. A crimson-shirt was on it. We had it first and ten on their thirty-three.

Jerry ran the option, faking a lateral to our

fullback, then tucking the ball under his arm to reverse his field and race down to the two before he was caught from behind.

"I'm watching this," Fitz said, "but I can't believe it. Pinch me, Johnny. I think I'm dreaming."

Instead of pounding at the middle of the Tiger's goal line defense Jerry faked to the fullback, bootlegged the football and sprinted around left end to score.

We kicked the point after this time and were leading 15-0.

When we'd kicked off to them again the Tigers began grinding out the yards toward our goal line. But the crimson-shirts grudged them every foot. When they had the ball on our five with a first down our middle linebacker came limping off the field.

"Hey, Coach." It was Jerry. "Let me in there."

I meant to say No. Instead I said, "All right, go ahead."

Our defense stiffened with Jerry back on the field. They held until it was fourth and a foot. Jerry called time out and came trotting over to the sidelines. "What do you think, Coach?"

"Quarterback sneak, maybe. But we've stopped them three times down the middle. What would you call?"

"A slant off tackle."

"Play it that way."

A fake to the fullback going into the line and a slant off tackle by their left halfback it was.

112

Jerry met him head-on and drove him back to the five.

I sent in a message with our offensive unit. Play it safe three downs and then kick out of there.

Jerry shouldered his way to the seven. The second play he was stopped for no gain. It was then he called a play I'd forgotten was in the book.

Taking the ball from our center Jerry raced deep in the end zone and whirled around to punt.

The Tigers were playing a seven man line with the four defensive backs close up to stop those middle of the line rushes. The quick kick worked to perfection. It hit on the forty and rolled to the forty-five before a crimson-shirt end covered it. There wasn't a blue-shirt near him.

Joe Nethery threw his hat on the ground and stamped on it.

Now Jerry began using our fullback and halfbacks, running right at that big Tiger line. Our linemen were doing some inspired blocking. Jerry ground out the yardage until it was first down on their fifteen. A Tiger end slugged him. That cost them half the distance to the goal. First and goal.

At this point we had a busted play. Fitz groaned when the fullback made his fake into the line but the halfback who was supposed to take the hand-off was blocking their left end instead.

Stuck with the ball, and with the whole Tiger line after him, Jerry ran for daylight and found some. Breaking three tackles he got around the end and into the end zone.

We kicked the conversion and were leading 22-0.

With first half time running out the Tigers came to life. In seven plays they marched the ball to a touchdown just as the gun sounded.

Joe Nethery elected to kick for the point after touchdown so we took a 22-7 lead into the locker room. Fitz and I also had an exhausted bunch of players. The Tiger touchdown march had proved that. The first team had played themselves out.

Only Jerry, sitting in a corner with his knees drawn up, looked fit enough to start the second half.

Joe was planning to massacre us during the long second half now that his team had momentum.

I let Fitz tell the boys how they could have stopped that Tiger touchdown march. "When they come at you with a power sweep you ends and tackles have to get rid of the interference so our defensive backs can get to the runner," he told them.

I had a quiet word with Jerry. "They're coming out to run all over us this next half," I told him. "But you know that."

Jerry nodded.

"Their coach will have them ready to defense the Wing T so here's what I want you to do. Start

114

running and passing off the Single Wing. When they adjust to that go back to the Wing T. Got it?"

"I've got it," Jerry said. "Football is a great game, isn't it?"

"You seem to be having a lot of fun out there."

"Yes, sir, I am," Jerry said.

To give my first team additional rest I started the second string except for Jerry when the Tigers received the second-half kickoff. Budd Sublet, Jerry's cousin, took the ball on his ten. Crossing the field to fake a hand-off to the other halfback he went down the sideline with a solid wall of blockers. Budd went into the end zone untouched. They kicked the point. Our lead had been whittled to 22-14.

"Hadn't we better take the second-stringers out?" Fitz asked.

It was a tough decision. I was tempted. Winning this game, however, was only one consideration. The way those second-stringers felt right now was another.

"Not yet," I told Fitz. "Let's give them a chance to get even. If we yank them now they'll come off the field heads down."

The kick-off went into the end zone. Jerry brought them out of the huddle into Single Wing formation on our twenty. He moved the team for a first down on the thirty-five before the Tigers adjusted. They stopped us then. We punted.

Those second-string ends smothered the re-

115

ceiver on their thirty yard line. Playing over their heads they proceeded to halt the Tigers march on our forty-five.

Jerry gathered in the punt on our five yard line and returned it to the twenty-five.

I sent our first team back into the game. The rest of the third quarter was a see-saw battle, both teams moving the ball but neither team able to score.

We had the ball on our own forty when Jerry opened the fourth quarter with a pass. His cousin picked it off and ran for a touchdown. This time they went for two and got the points with a quarterback sneak.

We had a tied ball game, 22-22.

"It was too good to last," Fitz said. "They'll murder us now."

The kick-off went into the end zone so Jerry started moving the team from the twenty. Running our backs and carrying himself on the option Jerry started a march. It was one of those "four yards in a cloud of dust" things. The Tigers weren't used to being pushed this way, especially by the team who hadn't won a game all season.

It got rough along the line. Penalties helped keep our drive going. But time was running out. It was on their thirty, third down, three to go, when there was another busted play. This time Jerry was clobbered by the middle guards and fumbled. The Tigers recovered. Their first play was a power sweep around our left end. The

Tiger halfback made it to mid-field before Jerry pulled him down from behind.

Their quarterback dropped back to pass.

Fitz and I had worked our boys hard on the pass rush. They came in on him but this quarterback was a good scrambler. But his mistake was trying to throw on the run. Jerry's receiver had him by a stride but the pass was short. Jerry gathered it in.

He ran diagonally across the field with a change of pace I couldn't believe. Seemingly trapped in front of our bench at the fifty yard line, Jerry pivoted, shook a tackler, reversed his field.

Now he was getting some blocks. He swerved downfield and went into the end zone stepping high.

We led 28-22. Jerry came over to consult me before the try for extra point or points. "Can we fake the kick and go for two?" he asked. "That interception shook them up."

The referee came over to give me the two-minute warning.

If we settled for seven points the Tigers could tie or beat us with a two point conversion.

"Go for two," I told him. "When you get your hands on that ball get into the end zone."

When I saw Jerry trotting back I knew I'd made a mistake. The play wouldn't work. Kneeling to hold the ball for the kicker Jerry wouldn't be able to move fast enough to avoid those big, crashing Tiger ends.

Yet we'd still have a six point lead.

Instead of running the ball Jerry simply stood up and rifled to Lou Weitzel over the fingertips of the Tiger line.

We had them 30-22.

We were playing a game team. When they took the kick-off their backs began cutting through our tired line like a hot knife through butter. They drove down to our twenty and with a beautiful pass off a reverse scored. That's when the gun went off.

The score stood 30-28. In our favor was the fact the Tigers now had to run or pass the ball if they wanted a 30-30 tie. Against us were eleven very tired crimson-shirted ball players.

Jerry huddled with our team. When the two teams faced each other I knew something was up. Our middle guards were shoulder to shoulder with Jerry only a step behind them.

The ball was snapped directly to their passer, the fullback. My guards cross-blocked, opening a hole for Jerry. He was on top of their fullback before he could cock his passing arm.

I stared at the scoreboard and rubbed my eyes. 30-28. "We upset the champions," I told Fitz.

"We didn't," he reminded me. "Our Monday morning quarterback got the job done for us."

118

29546 DRUGS AND YOU, by Arnold Madison. Illustrated with photographs. This straightforward account gives you basic information about the use and abuse of today's major drugs. (75¢)

29526 ALVIN FERNALD, FOREIGN TRADER, by Clifford B. Hicks. Illustrated by Bill Sokol. Alvin goes on a glorious but zany trip to Europe and gets involved with industrial spies. (75¢)

29770 PERPLEXING PUZZLES AND TANTALIZING TEASERS, by Martin Gardner. Illustrated by Laszlo Kubinyi. A fascinating collection of puzzles and teasers to challenge your wits, tickle your funny bone, and give you and your friends hours of entertainment. (95¢)

29311 LITTLE VIC, by Doris Gates. Illustrated by Kate Seredy. A young man's courageous struggle to qualify as a jockey and to ride the horse he loves to victory. (60¢)

29566 WHITE WATER, STILL WATER, by J. Allan Bosworth. Illustrated by Charles W. Walker. Swept down river on a raft, Chris faces a hazardous journey home through the wilderness— barefoot and equipped with nothing but a broken-bladed pocketknife. (75¢)

(If your bookseller does not have the titles you want, you may order them by sending the retail price, plus 25¢ (50¢ if you order two or more books) for postage and handling to: Mail Service Department, POCKET BOOKS, a division of Simon & Schuster, Inc., 1 West 39th Street, New York, N. Y. 10018. Please enclose check or money order—do not send cash.)